Sunshine and Shadows in Metropolitan Miami

Association of American Geographers

Comparative Metropolitan Analysis Project

Vol. 1   Contemporary Metropolitan America: Twenty Geographical Vignettes.
Cambridge: Ballinger Publishing Company, 1976.
Vol. 2.   Urban Policymaking and Metropolitan Dynamics: A Comparative Geo-
graphical Analysis. Cambridge: Ballinger Publishing Company, 1976.
Vol. 3.   A Comparative Atlas of America's Great Cities: Twenty Metropolitan
Regions. Minneapolis: University of Minnesota Press, 1976.

Vignettes of the following metropolitan regions are also published by Ballinger
Publishing Company as separate monographs:

- Boston
- New York-New Jersey
- Philadelphia
- Hartford-Central Connecticut
- Baltimore
- New Orleans

- Chicago
- St. Paul-Minneapolis
- Seattle
- Miami
- Los Angeles

Research Director:
John S. Adams, University of Minnesota

Associate Director and Atlas Editor:
Ronald Abler, Pennsylvania State University

Chief Cartographer:
Ki—Suk Lee, University of Minnesota

Steering Committee and Editorial Board:
Brian J.L. Berry, Chairman, University of Chicago
John R. Borchert, University of Minnesota
Frank E. Horton, Southern Illinois University
J. Warren Nystrom, Association of American Geographers
James E. Vance, Jr., University of California, Berkeley
David Ward, University of Wisconsin

Supported by a grant from the National Science Foundation.

Sunshine and Shadows in Metropolitan Miami

David B. Longbrake
Woodrow W. Nichols, Jr.
University of Miami

Ballinger Publishing Company ● Cambridge, Massachusetts
A Subsidiary of J.B. Lippincott Company

This book is printed on recycled paper.

International Standard Book Number: 0-88410-443-5

Library of Congress Catalog Card Number: 76-4792

Printed in the United States of America

Library of Congress Cataloging in Publication Data

Longbrake, David B
    Sunshine and shadows in Metropolitan Miami.

    Bibliography: p.
    1. Miami metropolitan area—Social conditions. 2. Anthropo-geography—Florida—Miami metropolitan area. 3. Miami metropolitan area—Economic conditions. 4. Urbanization—Florida. I. Nichols, Woodrow W., joint author, II. Title.
HN80.M53L66   309.1'759'38106   76-4792
ISBN 0-88410-443-5

Contents

List of Figures and Tables

List of Tables

Sunshine and
Shadows in
Metropolitan Miami

Introduction

The history of man parallels the development of cities. The drama that is human life has been staged in cities for centuries. What then is a city? What gives a city its vitality? What are the elements that add up to make a city? What are the variables that make one city exciting and another ordinary? Are cities artifically created or do they evolve in an organic fashion? Do cities require planning or do they just happen under the right circumstances? What is the quality of life that a city provides—that complex summation that means home?

No universal answer exists to the question of what a city is. In the words of Henry Churchhill, "the city is the people," and John Friedmann has said that "a city is the visible result of two processes, one physical and the other social, which interact to form the composite urban process."

These definitions may be useful in a general sense, but cities on an individual basis are really much more. To respond to an inquiry about Miami in a simple manner, one might say that Miami is a city of vibrant contrasts. Home of an inordinate share of the nation's obscenely rich and the prostrate poor, interna-

tional in flavor yet provincial in character, Miami is a city in search of an identity and maturity. But Miami is much more. It is a cultural center, a service center, an employment center. It is composed of many smaller subsystems and is itself a part of a larger system. In short, Miami is many things to different people.

The Miami study is presented in five parts. The first views the physical and economic components of the South Florida regional system. Attention then shifts to an overview of current trends in metropolitan Miami, a focal point of the South Florida region. Part two begins with a brief historical sequence but focuses on the present-day form and structure of urban Miami. Part three explores the six major geographic subareas within metropolitan Miami. Part four presents profiles of the social and cultural groups that give metropolitan Miami personality, character, and flavor unlike that of any other urban system. The final section summarizes metropolitan Miami's problems, indicates the policies for alleviating these problems, and takes a brief look at the prospects for the region.

An Overview

Urbanization can be defined in two ways: the movement of people from rural to urban areas that results in an increased proportion of the population living in urban rather than rural locations; and the spread of urban influences to rural areas thereby reducing the cultural differences between rural and urban populations. The state of Florida has played a significant role in the process of urbanization in the United States. Long regarded as a haven from urban problems found elsewhere in this country, it has been urbanizing at a rate exceeding that of the nation as a whole since the beginning of the twentieth century. Only about 20 percent urbanized in 1900, urban residents constituted 81 percent of Florida's population in 1970—7 percent above the national level.

In recent years the national population has begun to take on an older character, a factor that has and will continue to have profound implications for urban development in Florida. Currently, Florida is the ninth largest state and the recipient of a disproportionate share of the sixty-five and over age group (Figure 1). Looking ahead, there is little reason to doubt that the state will continue to grow in population. Migration occurs in response to changing economic, social, or political conditions. Migration based on amenities like climate and recreation is the most recent of the great migrations that have influenced growth and development in the United States. Spurred by growth in the tertiary or service sector of the economy, a decline in the propensity for industry to locate near markets and sources of raw materials, increasing incomes, research and development, and the increasing numbers and mobility of retirees, this so-called "amenities migration" began in the early 1950s and Florida became a favorite destination.

SOUTH FLORIDA

South Florida is much more than an area isolated at the southern tip of an elongated peninsula. It has a unique physical character and setting and is a functioning regional system with social, political, and economic elements. Its actual extent is somewhat vague, but includes the southern half of the state from Lake Okeechobee to Key West (Figure 2). The region contains such prominent features as a developed east coast, the Big Cypress Swamp and the Everglades in the west, and a flat porous limestone plain. However, climate and the Everglades are the most distinctive characteristics.

There is a relationship between South Florida's geographical location and its climate. Located nearer to the equator than any other part of the continental United States, its mild climate is influenced by the Gulf Stream ocean current passing within a few miles of Miami Beach, and the trade winds out of the southeast which warm the area in the winter and cool it in the summer. The climate is subtropical marine in character; summers are long, warm, and rainy followed by mild, dry

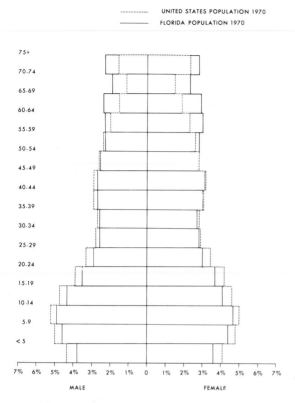

---------- UNITED STATES POPULATION 1970

———— FLORIDA POPULATION 1970

Figure 1. Percentage age distribution, 1940–1970.

winters. South Florida's climatic boundary is marked by recording stations whose thirty year records show all monthly mean temperatures above 64.4°F. Temperatures may appear high, but are moderated in summer months by sea breezes and frequent afternoon cloud cover. In winter, frosts have occurred in inland agricultural areas but rarely near the ocean. Another indication of the mild climate is the coconut palm which grows in great numbers along the coastal areas of South Florida. F. Page Wilson aptly summarized the virtues of South Florida's legendary climate when he answered the question of why the early pioneers liked Miami.

They liked the warmth and sunshine of its winters; the clean, cool, ozone-laden breeze which kept the long-drawn heat of summer from any real excess; its opportunities for sailing, swimming, fishing, for outdoor work and play throughout the year. This, they were sure, was a climate so different from others, so healthful, and benign, that thousands some day would come there to live.

Probably unique among the features giving South Florida its regional identity is the Florida Everglades. This natural system of flood-bloom-recession-concentration is a marvel of synchronization. Its life depends upon a direct supply of fresh water derived directly from rainfall which is retained briefly in what Arthur Marshall terms the Everglades waterway, the area of the Kissimmee-Okeechobee-Everglades basin. In its pristine condition, this strange waterway arose in the lakes of the upper Kissimmee River and flowed south via the meandering lower Kissimmee River to Lake Okeechobee. In wet years, the lake overspilled its southern rim into the sawgrass Everglades, adding that flow to the shallow sheetflow produced in the Everglades by direct rainfall. However, the greater part of the Everglades water has been lost to surface evaporation and evapotranspiration. Historically, the only significant surface flow to tide water from this system was at the tip of the peninsula into Florida Bay.

It is difficult for anyone who has not seen the Everglades to imagine its flatness (Figure 3). Slope within the basin from Lake Okeechobee to Florida Bay, a distance of more than 100 miles, averages about two inches per mile. This flatness, together with the friction of the dense marsh vegetation, produces a southerly surface flow rate of less than one-half mile per day.

Heavy tropical rains come to South Florida in the summer and fall. Throughout the Everglades waterway the water rises out of its shallow scattered lakes, rivers, ponds, and sloughs (Figure 4). It sheets over the southern Everglades marshes in the form of a very broad river which historically rose to seven or eight feet at summer flood.

Regenerative processes bloom with the rising spread of water under the warm summer sun. Plant germination and growth flourish as insects, crayfishes, killifishes, and reptiles reproduce at astounding rates. After the rains let up, the sheet water recedes into the deeper ponds and sloughs and concentrates the summer's reproduction of small organisms, making them available in essential densities to the waiting predators.

Over an eighty year period, many canals have been dug in the Everglades waterway for drainage and flood control purposes, diverting the fresh water more quickly to tide. The Everglades basin now has an elaborate plumb-

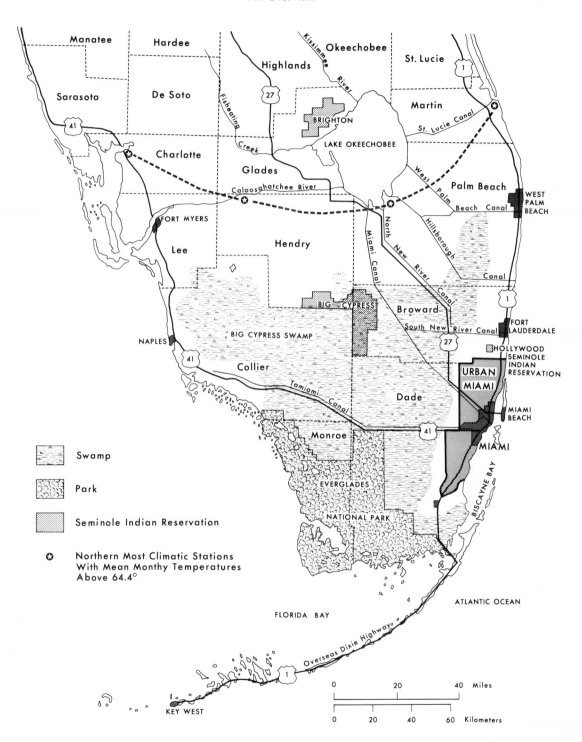

Figure 2. South Florida.

Figure 3. Florida Everglades during the dry winter season.

Figure 4. Florida Everglades during the wet summer season.

ing system with some 1,500 miles of canals plus levees, pumping stations, and assorted control structures draped liberally over the Everglades to control floods and supposedly to conserve its water. An inventory of the environmental effects of all this alternation includes:

- a gradual lowering of summer high water levels by about six feet in the sawgrass Everglades.

- reduction of the area of the Kissimmee marshlands by 65 percent and of the wetlands Everglades by about 50 percent;

- a drastic shortening of the surface flood period in Everglades National Park from six to eight months down to three or four;

- a decline in the order of 80 percent of the alligator population;

- the classification of twenty animals in the Department of Interior's Rare and Endangered Species list;

- rapid loss of organic muck soils (as much as an inch a year) in the agricultural area just south of Lake Okeechobee through atmospheric oxidation. The remaining life of this great peat and muck bed, a deltaic fan formed of decomposing marsh vegetation in the overspill from Lake Okeechobee over a 5,000 year span, is now estimated to be less than twenty-five years;

- the induction of salt water intrusion along the southeast coast brought about by lowering the head of fresh water in coastal aquifers.

The Everglades is more than just water, chemicals, mud, plants, fishes, and worms. It is an integrated life support system in which no part or function exists unto itself.

Besides the Everglades and the distinctive location and climate of South Florida the region is also a Daily Urban System focused on Miami and includes all those counties in which the proportion of resident workers who commute to Dade County exceeds the proportion who commute to other central counties.

METROPOLITAN MIAMI

The United States added twenty-four million persons during the 1960s, a 13 percent increase. This growth was not evenly distributed geographically. Metropolitan areas outpaced the nation as a whole, but urban areas located along the Great Lakes and the seacoasts have acquired a disproportionate share of the population increase.

Metropolitan Miami reflects this pattern. Settlement of Dade County began with a few villages and trading posts during the last quarter of the nineteenth century. By 1900, the total population was less than 5,000 residents. The arrival of rail transportation and the promotion of a winter paradise, together with successful trade and agricultural activities, generated a rapid urban growth after 1900, and population reached 100,000 by the mid-1920s.

The impact of the bust in the 1920s proved temporary. By the 1940s development of air transportation and the overall expansion of the American economy stimulated rapid urban growth in Florida once again.

From 1960 to 1970 the Miami SMSA (Dade County) grew by 35.6 percent, almost three times the national average. This single county absorbed over 18 percent of the total growth of the state of Florida, which increased 37 percent during this decade, from 4.9 million to 6.8 million. Among the thirty largest SMSAs, Miami in 1970 ranked twenty-fifth in total population (1,267,792). Of the total county growth in the last decade, nearly 76 percent was attributed to net migration and the remainder to natural increase. About 70 percent of the net migrants during the 1960s were Cuban refugees.

Until recently, rapid population growth was seriously questioned by only a few. It was generally considered a mark of economic and social dynamism and vitality. Even today large areas of the nation are still concerned with stimulating growth. However, it is now recognized that growth—especially when it is large scale, rapid, and relatively uncontrolled—carries new problems with it and exacerbates some old ones.

A major thesis of Alvin Toffler's best-selling book *Future Shock* is that the rate of change in modern society is not only rapid, but growing progressively faster to the point where many people are unable to make the mental and social adjustments required for survival. This same thesis can be applied equally well to the physical environment in which people live as growth pressures have exceeded nature's ability to adjust and maintain its ecosystems. Dade County, with its brief hundred year history as a settled community, is a good example of the problems described by Toffler.

However uncertain the future may be for metropolitan Miami, one need only examine present conditions and the factors which created them to judge what the future holds. Tremendous growth, both past and present, has contributed to this area's prosperity—but lies also at the root of many of its problems. If today can be looked upon as tomorrow's past, then an examination of present conditions points the way toward what needs to be done if the Miami region is to be a better place in which to live in the future.

CURRENT TRENDS

Population in Dade County increased by 322,745 people (35.6 percent) in the decade between the 1960 and 1970 census, while the amount of developed land in the county increased by approximately 31,000 acres (24.4 percent), primarily at the expense of the Everglades. Population density rose from 7.36 persons per developed acre in 1960 to 8.02 in 1970.

Expansion has been primarily toward the west, with lesser amounts to the north and south. A factor, other than population increase causing the spreading out of the built-up area of the Miami urban system, is the desirability of the suburbs and the easier access to them through better roads and expressways. Most of Dade County's expressway mileage has been built since 1960.

Comprehensive planning was introduced to Dade County with the organization of "METRO"—a metropolitan form of government—in the late 1950s (Table 1). The first land use plan was adopted in Dade County in 1965, but the population of the county by this time was well in excess of one million and vast amounts of land had already been developed. Evaluation of unplanned growth in urban Miami from 1890 through the early 1960s is difficult, but many recent problems illustrate the impact of decisions or neglect twenty, thirty, or even forty years ago (Figure 5).

Vanishing beaches are but one example of this negative impact (Figure 6). Late in the 1960s, the U.S. Army Corps of Engineers revealed a plan to "save" Miami Beach, calling for building an artificial beach in front of the original shoreline which has been slowly disappearing as a result of erosion processes. The plan required substantial monetary investment but gave no assurance that the erosion process could be completely controlled. Nevertheless, the plan at least offered a new beach, the opportunity to monitor change, and the possibility of developing a beach maintenance program. The plan was never implemented.

Careful research of documents related to the development of Miami Beach fails to reveal any efforts to preserve and maintain the beaches or even a serious concern for this the most valuable of the city's assets. The preparation of design and construction standards conducive to a rational use of this precious natural resource are nonexistent. In fact, critics claim that beach destruction has actually been accelerated by the manner in which hotels were built.

The use of water provides another example of the negative environmental impact of unplanned growth. Water-based activities have long been one of South Florida's main attractions, but in 1972 only two canals in a network of more than twenty were still suitable for swimming. Even the Miami River, which passes through the heart of Miami, is still unsafe for human contact despite remarkable clean-up efforts by state and local authorities.

Still another example in Dade County is the current water supply crisis. The typical flat lowland terrain of Dade County, matched with an unusual geologic formation, results in a water table just a few feet below the surface. This situation, combined with sandy soils, creates conditions that make it difficult to build on the land without altering natural processes and conditions. To avoid contamination of the shallow aquifer requires sizable capital investments to provide for sewage and drainage.

Preservation of fresh water supplies is not a characteristic feature of unplanned growth. Thus, no plans or requirements of any kind were drawn up for simultaneously managing the environment and accommodating urban development in Dade County during the early period of growth. This lack of control has been re-

Table 1. Allocation of Selected Functions in Metro-Dade*

County Functions	Mixed Functions	City-Controlled Functions
Highways	Waste Disposal	Waste Collection
Arterials	Water	Street Cleaning and Roadside Main-
Bridges	Sewerage	tenance
Arterial street lighting	Distribution lines	Streets and Neighborhood
Traffic engineering	Treatment-Outfall	Street Lighting
Airport	Libraries	Legal Services
Administrative Services	Fire	Parks and Recreation
Tax assessment	Protection	Police
Tax collection	Communications	Traffic regulation code—enforce-
Water Transport and Terminals	Training	ment, protection, and patrol
Gas	Police	
Sewerage	Harbor patrol	
Regulation	Communications	
Planning	Alcohol test exam	
Health and Public Welfare	Housing Code—Enforcement	
General welfare	Building Code—Enforcement	
Hospital		
Nursing homes		
Public health		
Alcohol rehabilitation		
Water pollution control		
Air pollution control		
Traffic Courts		
Police		
Training		
Detention-Corrections		
Criminal justice information system		
Crime prevention		
Crime reporting		
Accident reporting		

Source: Edward Sofen, *The Miami Metropolitan Experiment* (Garden City, N.Y.: Doubleday Anchor, 1966), 2nd ed., pp. 135–39; and Aileen Lotz and Thomas J. Wood, "Dade County, Florida," (Working paper prepared February 21, 1974 for Rann Research Project, University of Miami, Center for Urban and Regional Studies).

sponsible for the indiscriminate construction of canals for drainage and dredging of lakes to obtain fill materials. As a result of these practices, billions of gallons of fresh water rush to the ocean. The delicate flow system developed over centuries has been broken, and all of South Florida's ecosystems have been affected. In addition, drainage from septic tanks in sandy soils has contributed to the pollution of well fields, drainage canals, rivers, and ultimately Biscayne Bay. Some 40 percent of Dade County's housing units in 1970 are still not hooked up to a public sewer system.

In addition to population growth and the physical development of land with its associated environmental impact, metropolitan Miami is experiencing and has undergone several widespread changes since 1960. Well over a quarter million Latins, most of them refugees from Castro's Cuba, settled here. The rigid boundaries which contained the black ghettos of Liberty City, Brownsville, South Miami, and Coconut Grove were breached in places and extensive communities shifted from white to black occupancy. The house-building industry changed from predominantly single family subdivision construction to apartments and condominiums of all sizes. Both high rises and condominiums were virtually unseen before 1960. There was also a significant change in the form of urban expansion as more intensive larger scale developments replaced the sprawling single family subdivision projects of the 1950s. The economy continued to expand enough to keep pace with the need for jobs, and per capita income increased slightly faster in metropolitan Miami than it did in the state or nation.

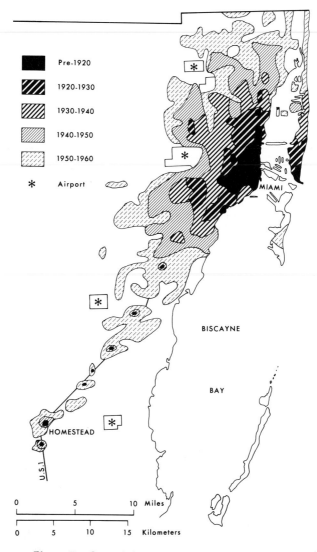

Figure 5. Growth in urban Miami, 1920–1960.

In its quest for maturity, Miami sometimes appears to have greater success replicating the problems rather than the assets of other larger cities. Thus, population and the economy were not the only things growing in recent years; so were some serious problems. Crime rates more than doubled between 1960 and 1970. Drug abuse reached epidemic proportions, particularly among the youth. Black families were better off financially than in 1960, but still earned only 57 percent of non-Latin white median family incomes. School age children of every color from poor areas were failing to at-

tain the same level of scholastic achievement in reading and arithmetic scores as were children from affluent areas.

Miami was the only major metropolitan area in the country whose overcrowded housing rate rose substantially during the 1960s. Although much of the crunch was felt by Latins, blacks were no better off in 1970 than they were in 1960 and in some places they were worse off. The poor and many not-so-poor were paying ever increasing proportions of their income for housing, making housing costs one of the top problems in Dade County. In addi-

Figure 6. Miami Beach at low tide.

tion, development upon development has been added to the residential stock of Dade County without any provision for parks or open land. Despite encouraging decreases in infant mortality rates among blacks, their rate was still about double the infant mortality rate among whites. Moreover, the 1970 death rate among blacks between the ages of twenty and sixty-five also remained twice that of whites.

Industrial activities have begun to complement the influence of tourism on Dade County's economy. Yet problems related to facility location, buffer zones, and poorly designed sites are of increasing concern and affect many industrial developments in Dade County. A recent survey indicates serious blighting influences generated by developments which properly located and designed would have meant positive rather than negative elements in the growth of urban Miami.

Residents and visitors experience the Dade County transportation crisis at least twice a day. Lack of planning during the period of rapid growth is largely responsible for insufficient rights of way for many existing roads and the absence of reserved lands for facilities that should have been planned years ahead of today's needs. Right of way acquisition and displacement and relocation of families and businesses are typical problems throughout the nation. They are especially typical of older cities developed well before the automobile, but could have been avoided in Dade County, which had less than 100,000 population at the beginning of the automobile era.

The above represent several prominent problems and trends currently affecting the physical environment and quality of life in metropolitan Miami. Issues related to the general problems of deficient environmental quality, improper level of services, and inadequacy of the urban infrastructure stemming from rapid and unplanned urban growth could easily be extended for many pages.

The experience of Dade County must be remembered not as a base for planning the future and expanding current trends, but as a reference for avoiding the errors of unplanned growth which lead to the waste and destruction of our precious natural resources. Experience should help us to define an approach to urban problems with imaginative and forward-looking ideas that will correct present problems and eventually create a better environment for urban society. Dade County is now in the process of formulating policies that hopefully will shape the process of urbanization in Miami along more satisfactory lines.

Processes, Parts, and the Whole

Understanding metropolitan Miami requires knowledge of its historical growth processes, the individual components of the system, and the patterns that have emerged. A succession of different cultural groups and the ways they changed Miami, the pros and cons of metropolitan government, the economy, public health, education, recreation, and the various urban patterns, such as transportation, housing, poverty, and crime are all examined here to illustrate the interrelationships that produce order within the Miami system.

HISTORICAL GROWTH

Through time, Indians, Spanish, British, and twentieth century Americans have each played significant roles in transforming Miami from a region of wilderness into a vast metropolitan area. In 1567, when the first recorded attempt was made to establish a non-Indian settlement in the region, the southern part of the Florida peninsula was the home of two related native tribes who had resided in the area for more than 1,500 years. The western portion belonged to the Calusa, while the east coast from Cape Kennedy to the Keys was the home of several small independent tribes. The Tequesta on Biscayne Bay was the most prominent of these latter groups and the first to transform the Miami environment.

The subsequent arrival and settlement of individuals and groups began when Pedro Mendez was commissioned by Spain in 1565 to colonize Florida. Approximately two years later, Mendez reached the Miami area and established a Jesuit mission, a garrison, and a fort among the Tequesta for the Spaniards.

Little remains of the recorded history between the settlement of the Jesuits and the occupation by the British in 1763. Under the Treaty of Paris, Florida was ceded to England which made the first recorded land grant in 1774. King George dispensed land according to the recipient's military position or civilian status. He charged inhabitants to protect the rights of the Indians, and restricted them from the Indian hunting grounds.

The end of the Revolutionary War in 1783 paved the way for more Spanish settlement in the Miami area. In this last period of Spanish occupation five land grants totaling 2,735 acres were made on the lower east coast from 1783 to 1821. This Spanish period came to an end in 1812 when President Monroe appointed General George Matthews and Colonel John McKee to negotiate with the Spanish government for the possession of Florida. The "Republic of Florida" was the result after insurgents forced Monroe's negotiators to withdraw. The republic lasted four years, and five years later (1821) the United States finally succeeded in annexing Florida.

Under the Treaty of Ildefonso, the U.S. recognized the five land grants made by the Spanish government. Most of these properties were acquired by R.R. Fitzpatrick, who erected buildings, imported slaves to work the cotton plantations, and cleared the bayfront of hammock in the vicinity of the Miami River from

North Miami to Coconut Grove, planting lime and other tropical fruit trees.

The Seminole War (1835) interfered with Fitzpatrick's slave property, so he fled to Key West. Subsequently, the United States Army settled on the land and named it Fort Dallas. During the following year (1836) Dade County was incorporated, named in honor of Major Francis L. Dade, who was massacred by the Seminole Indians near Bushnell in Sumpter County.

The Incorporation of Miami

The Seminole War ended in 1842, but Fitzpatrick, who had become seriously involved financially because of the war, was forced to convey his holdings to his nephew William F. English, who neglected the property and eventually sold it. From then on the lands changed hands several times.

By 1890 a small settlement had grown up around Fort Dallas, one of six population clusters in the region—the others being Coconut Grove, Miami, Buena Vista, Lemon City, and Little River (Figure 7). Most of these settlements were engaged in various forms of agriculture, which focused heavily on tomato crops along country roads from the large Little River and Arch Creek section in the north to Larkins (now South Miami), Perrine, and the new settlement of Homestead in the south. Fruit growing was also important, most of it in grapefruit groves west and south of Miami and bordering the Coconut Grove area. Other fruits—especially mangos and avacados—were plentiful in the southwest and remnants of these groves can still be seen throughout the southern region of the county.

Agriculture has also played an important role in the growth and development of metropolitan Miami. The severe freeze in the winter of 1894–1895, which killed most of Florida's citrus except in Dade County, is credited as one of the major factors used by landowner Julia D. Tuttle to convince Henry M. Flagler that he should push his railroad line further down the coast from West Palm Beach. Tuttle made a trip to see Flagler and promised to hand over half of her extensive acreage if he would extend his railroad to Fort Dallas. At first he refused, but after the Big Freeze, when the ice was reported to be an inch thick in some parts of northern Florida, Tuttle sent Flagler flowers to prove that Miami was below the

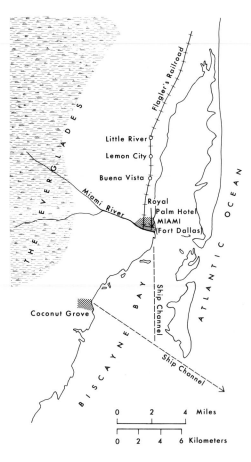

Figure 7. Miami in 1900.

freezing line. Flagler agreed to build the railroad, started work immediately, and completed it on April 15, 1896, approximately three and one-half months before the city was legally incorporated.

The Impact of Flagler

Even though agriculture was a major stimulus in bringing the railroad to Miami, the railroad itself had an even greater impact. One month after the first trains reached Miami, Flagler began publishing the city's first newspaper, the *Miami Metropolis*. In mid-January 1897 Flagler's Royal Palm Hotel opened its doors on the north bank at the mouth of the Miami River. Later Flagler extended his railroad to Homestead and then to Key West. This "railroad that went to the sea," had 106 miles built practically over water. It was destroyed by the Labor Day hurricane in

1935, but U.S. Highway 1 was constructed in part with remnants of the original trestle work.

Other projects related directly or indirectly to Flagler were clearing, grading, and paving Flagler Street and Miami Avenue; a sewer system which emptied into the Miami River and Biscayne Bay; rental housing units, mostly in the form of cottages two blocks south of Flagler Street; the opening and improvement of the Royal Palm Hotel, the most successful of the five hotels in the area; harbor improvement and the completion of the S.S. *Miami* (a steamship); and a street light system, a city hall, and a jail.

Before Flagler's railroad, most of Miami was devoted to agriculture to sustain the local inhabitants. However, after the arrival of the railroad, there was a shift in emphasis away from local markets to export production. The railroad period saw an immediate increase in the revenues obtained from the tourist trade and many service functions on both sides of Miami Avenue soon developed, along with other businesses and professional practices.

Land Development

In approximately eighty years, Miami has grown from five scattered settlements containing about 400 persons to a vast urban system composed of twenty-six municipalities and more than 1.5 million residents. Traditionally, land development has taken two directions in the state of Florida. One was influenced by a "spirit of the new frontier," and the other was simply increments to existing settlements.

Developments of the new frontier variety were initially guided by tourism and land speculation and have had a major impact on settlement patterns in South Florida. The incremental pattern is more representative of urban growth in and around older cities in northern Florida and in northern cities. In recent years a third land development pattern based on "new community" and "planned unit development" concepts has emerged in Florida in response to an increasing awareness of the problems and limitations inherent in the earlier practices of land development. Today large scale development practices are the predominant form of urban growth in South Florida and Miami.

The railroad was one of the earliest forces generating significant land development in the state. Each new station during the construction period nurtured new settlements or promoted the growth of existing ones. Flagler's railroad inched toward the southern tip of the peninsula providing a land transportation link with the north. When it reached the mouth of the Miami River, it augmented Miami's role as a transfer point for produce and tourists to and from sailing vessels and steamships.

The importance of the Miami River was also realized during this early period of development. Located just south of the initial settlement, it became the focal point of the region with its excellent docking space, ease of navigation, and outlet to Biscayne Bay.

While rail and water transportation provided the major stimulus for growth between 1896 and 1910, the automobile took over this role in the decade from 1910 to 1920, as the population quadrupled to 42,750. Along with an increase in tourism, the automobile permitted low density development which soon covered much of the northern part of Dade County. It also played a role in the development of Miami Beach after John Collins, the original developer of Miami Beach, built the Venetian Causeway for automobile access, triggering an explosion of tourism on the beach.

In the years following World War I, transportation advances, economic prosperity, and well-organized promoters equipped with an army of trained salesmen marked the beginning of the real boom era of land devleopment in Miami. The era proved to be the most heralded and controversial one in the history of southern Florida.

Real estate developers devised grandiose schemes to sell land to new residents who could spend their already accumulated capital on permanent or seasonal residences. They used planned residential satellite cities to attract buyers, telling them they could escape from congestion and other environmental ills and still reside close to urban services.

Much of the development in Miami through the years has taken place during a series of great land booms, with the sometimes carnival atmosphere of the speculator's fantasy world having a strong influence on the character of present-day Miami. The first boom took place in 1925 when nattily dressed land speculators known as "binder boys" bought acreage for 5 percent down and peddled it on the street at enormous profits. One realtor went as far as suggesting that only two types of people live in the United

States—those living in Miami and those wanting to live in Miami.

The more knowledgeable and responsible developers surveyed the land first, platted subdivisions or communities, and then began their sales programs, making few if any improvements on their sites. The pattern followed by the vast majority of land developers was to subdivide and plat the land, and then start construction on some type of building or project which the developer felt would serve as a catalytic agent in setting off a sales and building boom. Promotional structures and schemes conceived by the boom barons included hotels, Moorish and Spanish development themes, and exotic street names (Figure 8). All too often these grandiose and garish structures were never completed.

Occasionally, as was the case in Coral Gables, Miami Shores, and a few others, profits from land sales were invested in project improvements, thus generating the beginnings of a durable and pleasant urban atmosphere. But for the most part, the boom era was a period of land speculation, rapid sales, and resales.

Legal regulations on land development during this period were varied, but focused mainly on the regulations of sales and to a limited extent on the control of land subdivision. As an illustration, the city of Miami adopted a regulation in 1925 forbidding the completion of real estate deals on the sidewalks. Regulations in terms of minimum standards for open space, roads, or facilities were minimal or virtually nonexistent.

During the boom period, population in Miami increased to 143,000, and downtown Miami enjoyed a building surge. The consequences of overspeculation and oversubdi-

Figure 8. Moorish theme land promotional structure in Opa Locka now serving as Opa Locka's city hall.

vision were felt in 1926 when the boom turned into a bust. This was further aggravated by a disastrous hurricane which left Miami practically helpless. By 1930 the overall development of the area was disjointed and ailing, with many underdeveloped gaps.

The stock market crash intensified the crash of Miami's real estate market and the Depression of the 1930s brought all forms of land development to a halt. The newly formed tourist industry and the introduction of air transportation helped reawaken the Miami land development. Toward the end of the decade tourists once again were flocking to Miami in great numbers. Employment expanded because the tourist business needed workers, many of whom lived in the expanding satellite communities.

Land development this time was undertaken on a much smaller scale and activity centered on the construction of small hotels and single family houses. There was little interest in developing strong controls for the land development process in Miami. But gradually a number of communities such as Coral Gables, Miami Shores, and Miami Springs began adopting zoning ordinances to guide the renewed growth of the period and to preserve and enhance the quality of the emerging communities.

World War II kept the growth of Miami at a moderate pace in the early 1940s, but the postwar years brought another tourist boom. Servicemen who had brought their families to the area and other migrants working in military installations on Miami Beach subsequently relocated to other parts of the county. After the war the demand for housing increased sharply. As housing demand exceeded supply and airport industries and educational facilities grew, the overall development of the city was strengthened. This new development was accompanied by a comprehensive plan for drainage and flood control in the Everglades that eventually opened up new agriculture lands, urban expansion, and the Everglades National Park as a recreational and tourist attraction.

Two new breeds of entrepreneurs emerged. Some individuals or organizations acquired land for sale or formed associations with contract builders. In addition, large firms for the first time began putting together complete service packages of finance, construction, and sales under the auspices of a single organization.

These two types of land development operation have been responsible for most of the housing units built after World War II. Fully 380,690 units or more than 85 percent of Miami's total housing in 1970 has been constructed since 1940.

Traditional constraints on land development in the Miami area include the ocean; Biscayne Bay; the Everglades National Park; and poorly drained lowlands, the latter of which can be overcome by drainage and filling. The largest area of recent development has been along the Palmetto Expressway near the Miami International Airport and includes a number of industrial sites. Another large area of development has been the expansion along the main thoroughfares westward toward the Everglades—Tamiami Trail, Bird Road, and North Kendall Drive. This area represents the western spread of urbanized Miami and contains mainly single family residential units, including townhouses and garden apartments.

Expansion in South Dade County has been primarily along U.S. 1 (Dixie Highway), with additional developments at the edge of Biscayne Bay along Old Cutler Road. However, South Dade is poised for a potentially dramatic change in land development patterns. Serviced by only a single transportation spine (U.S. 1), development in South Dade has been severely inhibited by lack of access and resulting traffic congestion. The recently completed southern extension of the Florida Turnpike will alter this situation significantly by providing a new access corridor within the area. This new link to the metropolitan transportation network may well give violent vent to the pent-up demand for housing in South Dade.

Few large tracts of land remain undeveloped in the northern portions of Dade County as most of the land lying in the path of northward expansion has already succumbed to the developers' bulldozers. In fact, the current wave of land development has already penetrated northward into the southern reaches of Broward County. Residential growth has dominated the northern section of Dade County with some industrial build-up along the major highways.

PEOPLE, GOVERNMENT, AND ACTIVITY SYSTEMS

The previous section explained how land development has influenced the general structure of the Miami SMSA. Let us turn now to the people, the government, and the activity systems in the Miami region and their interrelationships. To the casual observer Miami, like any vast urban area, may appear chaotic. Residential land use may appear to have developed where it did without any apparent plan or reason; the rapid population growth in certain parts of the area and the net increase throughout the years might seem to have taken place overnight; movement of people and commodities might seem to occur spontaneously in all forms and at all times of the day; twenty-six municipalities and a county government may be viewed as haphazard and confusing; and the numerous economic, social, and recreational activities on the landscape might seem highly disordered. However, much to the contrary, the order is present, if hidden. The components work together in an integrated urban system.

People

The people came first, 1,267,792 of them in 1970. Compared to the other nineteen SMSAs in this series, certain unique characteristics emerge with respect to Miami's inhabitants. Among the twenty SMSAs Miami has the highest rankings for percentage foreign born; percentage of Spanish-language persons; percentage over sixty-five years of age; median age; crime; and crowding measured by percentage of housing units with more than 1.51 persons per room. Miami also had high rankings for median contract rent (third); death rate (third), reflecting in large part the overall age character of the population; and percentage of persons below the poverty level (second).

Low rankings characterize Miami's percentage employed in manufacturing (eighteenth); median family income (nineteenth); and share of families earning more than $15,000 per year (eighteenth). Lowest rankings are recorded for fertility and birth rates (twentieth) and percentage in the under eighteen age group (twentieth), again reflecting the concentration of elderly. On other scores, Miami is near average in such areas as education levels; percentage of females in the labor force; percentage of males unemployed; percentage employed in white collar occupations; percentage of black population; median value of owner-occupied housing; and percentage of housing units in single family structures.

One of the unique characteristics of urban Miami is its ethnic composition. In 1970 residents were divided into three main ethnic groups—15 percent black; 24 percent Spanish-speaking; and 61 percent non-Latin whites.

Although the county's 190,000 blacks reside in North, Central, and South Dade, they are concentrated in relatively small areas (Figure 9).

According to the census definition, a person is Spanish-speaking if he had a parent whose mother tongue was Spanish or if he lives in a family in which either the head or spouse reported Spanish as the mother tongue. The county's 299,000 Spanish-language residents were originally concentrated in the downtown Little Havana area but then dispersed to the west and northwest to Hialeah. By comparison South and Northeast Dade have very few Spanish-speaking residents although Spanish-speaking people are generally more dispersed than blacks.

The median age for blacks in Dade County in 1970 was 21.5 years, down from 27.4 in 1940 and 23.5 in 1960. For Spanish-speaking persons the 1970 median age was 32.2, and for non-Latin whites, 39.8 years. For Spanish-speaking persons the explanation for the high median may lie with the selective characteristics of the Cuban immigration. Middle class Cubans who disagreed with Castro did not want to see their children raised in an educational system strongly influenced by his policies. Therefore, families in these age categories and positions were much more likely to emigrate than were those without any children or preschool children.

The youthful composition of Dade County's black population is due to the characteristics of their birth and mortality rates. Among the 1970 black population, 48 percent were less than twenty years old, compared to 35 percent for Latins and 28 percent for other whites. The black fertility rate was 3.6, compared to the Latin rate of 2.1.

Education levels for Dade County are close to average, with a median of 12.1 years of school completed compared to a national average for large cities of 12.2. Once again, however, there are notable disparities between the ethnic elements. The typical non-Latin white has completed 12.3 years of school, the typical Latin resident has 10.4 years of

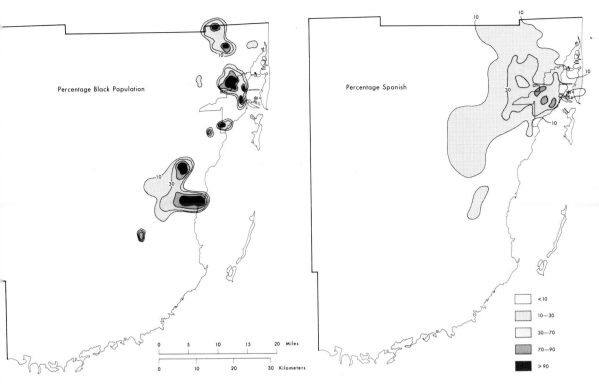

Figure 9. Ethnic Distribution in Urban Miami.

school, and the typical black only 9.4 years. Over 12 percent of non-Latin whites aged twenty-five and older hold college degrees or better. Yet the 10 percent of the Latins with college degrees far outpace the 4 percent of the blacks who have reached this level of education. Also, only about 12 percent of non-Latin whites aged twenty-five and over have just an elementary school education compared to 31 percent for Latins and 38 percent for blacks.

Considering the discrepancies between ethnic groups in educational levels, it is not surprising to find corresponding disparities in their economic situation. Median 1969 family income for Dade County was $9,245, but was $10,477 for non-Latin white families, $8,091 for Latins, and $5,983 for blacks. While 45 percent of all families earn more than $10,000, 53 percent of non-Latin white families exceed this amount, compared to 36 percent of Latin families and 20 percent of black families. About 9 percent of non-Latin white families were below the census-established poverty level, while 15 percent of Latin families and

32 percent of the black families failed to reach above the 1969 poverty line.

Metropolitan Governance

In 1957, Dade County and its twenty-six municipalities created a two tier form of government in which certain areawide services were allocated to Metro (the county) and others to the individual municipalities. A metropolitan form of government was possible for various reasons—the mobility of population, tourist atmosphere, no-party system, weak position of labor and minority groups, vulnerable past of the central city, and the strong dependence of the population on the areawide newspapers for political leadership. In addition, Dade County's early success with consolidation of health, hospital, school, and port authority helped pave the way for more extensive political integration.

Since the creation of the Metro, attention has shifted away from the debate between local autonomists and consolidationists and toward issues such as taxation, representation, and the division of governmental functions. A central issue is the proper division of functions between the county and the municipalities. This concern developed partly because a clear-cut division of functions was not stated in Metro's charter. Metro has the power to "set reasonable minimum standards for all governmental units for the performance of any service or function," and is empowered to do almost anything that is necessary to carry on a central metropolitan government. Various municipalities have challenged this power—for example, Miami Shores in 1958 regarding its traffic code; the 1967 Coral Gables' allegation of double taxation with respect to fire protection; and the city of Miami's efforts in 1962 to gain urban renewal powers of their own in redeveloping the Central District. In these instances, it was ruled that Metro superseded all municipal charters, that municipalities cannot be exempted from county taxation for services that are offered on a countywide basis even though the municipality does not choose to use them, and that renewal should be handled by Metro.

Most areawide functions are handled at the metropolitan level. Electrical power is franchised to Florida Power and Light which provides electricity to all areas except Homestead, which has its own. Water and sewage, despite the Water and Sewer Authority, is provided by the county, the cities, or not at all (see Table 1).

Many functions are handled at the Metro level because some municipalities find it more economical to let Metro handle them, especially the smaller ones. Other municipalities generaly oppose Metro initiatives—for example, Miami Beach, Hialeah, Miami Shores, and Homestead. Antagonism is usually reflected in their reluctance to surrender functions to Metro. Still others, such as South Miami, which requested a Metro takeover of its fire department in 1966 so that it could meet the maximum millage rate, have retained the quality of their services by surrendering them to Metro. Some functions Metro has been reluctant to accept. For example, waste collection is one of the few services that has never been seriously discussed in terms of a city to county transfer.

Zoning, parks and recreation, and police protection are clearly municipal functions, even though the county can exercise an option to adopt a countywide zoning ordinance.

Some municipalities have partially transferred police patrol functions and park and recreation functions to Metro. Thus, rather than a rigid two tier form of government, there appears to be a great deal of interaction and cooperation within a rather stable metropolitan political process. Generally, problems seldom arise unless the county tries to assume a function that all or some cities have previously provided. There have been confrontations, such as Metro's abolition of the Miami Housing Authority, but Metro's absorption of functions has been rather limited due to administrative, financial, and other factors. Metro is the dominant governmental force in the Miami SMSA; however, the issues are currently shifting from Metro versus the cities to Metro versus the people. Issues include the division of functions, representation, and the distribution of taxes and spending.

Activity Systems

Transportation. To what extent have the desires of users of the Miami transportation system and the community at large been fulfilled? The users of the Miami transportation system worry about three things—traffic congestion travel times, operating costs, and safety. Traffic congestion in Miami results from two factors—rapid population growth; and the nature of its economy, which brings millions of tourists and other businesses to the area. In response to this problem, there have been recent attempts to expand both the external and internal transportation networks. Miami International Airport, the port of Miami, the Seaboard Coast Railroad, and Amtrak constitute the most important external components. The overcrowding problem is most acute at Miami International Airport and the port of Miami. Responses include more parking space, additional concourses, and increasing rental services at Miami International Airport; studies to find a suitable location for a new jetport; and the discussion of another deep-water port, possibly in the southern part of the county.

Internally, the street and expressway system has been designed to accommodate the automobile and the county's bus systems, but the streets and expressways are severely overcrowded. Buses are slow and plagued by transfers between bus routes. Attempts to bring an end to these problems include new expressways and the 1972 voter approval of a $132.5 million bond issue to provide the local share of a new rapid transit system.

The proposed expressway and rapid transit systems will stimulate land development in certain parts of the SMSA, but it is questionable whether the environment will be improved if the population continues to grow as it has in the past, or that the needs of the poor and elderly will be met by the rapid transit system scheduled to be completed in 1985. Skeptics argue that the number of vehicle trips will be so great by 1985 that the new rapid transit system will be rendered obsolete upon completion.

Health Care. The problems surrounding health care in Miami are the same as elsewhere—spiraling costs of hospital and physician care, some misplacement of primary care physicians, and health care needed in places where none is provided. Between 1971 and 1972 alone there was an 8 percent average increase in the cost of a private room in thirty-one of thirty-eight hospitals; the rates for a semiprivate room increased 7 percent during the same period in thirty-three of thirty-eight hospitals. Physician fees also increased substantially.

By most standards, Miami meets the requirement in terms of having enough physicians, but it falls short in terms of their offices being readily accessible to everyone. Primary care physicians tend to cluster close to commercial areas where office space is greater and/or near hospitals (Figure 10). Such locations make it difficult for some persons, especially the poor and elderly in outlying areas, to reach their physicians without having to pay substantial transportation costs.

Accessibility to public and private facilities also varies throughout Miami. There are thirty-seven nursing homes, eleven homes for the aged, and ten homes designed for special health services; many of these are located outside the areas that contain the greatest concentration of persons needing such services. One of the policies of the Health Planning Council of South Florida is that of decentralizing health care to bring facilities closer to neighborhoods, especially the black ghettos. Just as in other American cities, emphasis is shifting away from the hospital as the preeminent unit in the health delivery system. The hospital orientation as the source of both medical training and

medical care has dominated American medicine for more than two generations. The inability of the hospital to handle a growing diversity of health care needs, ranging from a changing social environment to the development of new health insurance programs, has led to an emphasis on the expansion of neighborhood health care centers.

Dade County is responding to the call by decentralizing ambulatory care away from emergency rooms and into health care complexes in various regions within the metropolitan area. Four such facilities were approved in a 1972 general obligation bond issue. Supplementary neighborhood health centers have been established in the Model City area, the area south of 36th Street near the Miami River, Little Havana, South Beach, Coconut Grove, and Goulds. In addition, the County Health Department maintains nine public health units. Services include maternal and infant child care, family planning, diagnosis and treatment of venereal disease and tuberculosis, immunization, dentistry, public health nursing, and health education.

Education. The Miami public school system of 236 schools and approximately 235,000 pupils ranks as the sixth largest in the nation. There are six major colleges and universities, as well as many technical and professional schools. The salient aspects of the educational system are desegregation and the Cuban impact on both the public school system and higher education.

The history of desegregation in the public schools of Miami parallels that of other systems. Desegregation began in 1959 when Orchard Villa and Air Base Elementary became the first integrated public schools in Miami and the state of Florida. From this beginning, desegregation slowly evolved to its present situation, which finds four of twenty senior high, eight of thirty-nine junior high, and fifty-eight of one hundred and seventy-two elementary schools still predominantly black.

The other major change in the educational system took place with the Cuban influx. By October 1965 there were 21,288 Spanish-speaking pupils in the public schools or 10.5 percent of the total enrollment. In response to the new residents' lack of English and the need for continued instruction in Spanish, two programs—English as a second language

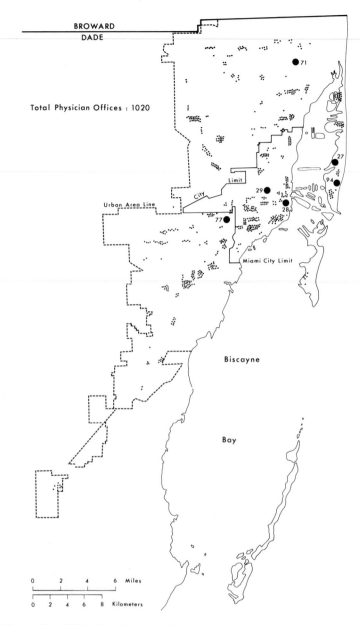

Figure 10. Office locations of primary care physicians in private practice.

and Spanish as a first or second language—have been implemented. In addition, substantial numbers of Cubans are enrolled in the major colleges and universities within the area.

Open Space and Recreation. In 1969 the Dade County Planning Department and the Parks and Recreation Department made sev-

eral recommendations for developing open space and recreation facilities, beautifying the total environment, and preserving open space. Beginning with the standard of 4.5 acres of open space per 1,000 persons the Community Improvement Program of Dade County has evaluated each locale. Exceptionally well-served areas are Coral Gables, South Miami, Key Biscayne, South Miami Beach, and southern Dade. The central portions of Miami, north and south of the Miami River, are the areas least adequately served by public open space. Of the major areas containing no public open space at all, most are located in the northwestern and southern parts of the county. In all, more than 592,000 persons are either not served or inadequately served by public open space. Tourists prefer to use the beaches, the bay and ocean for fishing and boating, and the golf courses; therefore, the lack of submetropolitan parks is primarily a problem for the permanent Dade resident.

METROPOLITAN PATTERNS

The Economy

Metropolitan Miami has a trade and service economy geared to tourism and the provision of goods and services to an increasing population (Figure 11). The labor force and employment levels increased faster than the population from 1960 to 1970. Participation in the labor force is less than the national rate, but white females are increasing their participation significantly. Unemployment follows national trends, fluctuating from 6.0 percent in 1972 to 4.1 percent in late 1972, and is highest in the black population.

Between 1960 and 1970 jobs in agriculture, forestry, and fisheries declined about 1 percent while manufacturing and services gained more than two percent each. Manufacturing has shown an increase since 1965 and there is

speculation that the trend will continue. Apparel is the largest manufacturing industry, followed by fabricated metal products and food products. The dominant sectors in Dade's economy are service and trade. Even though their size is large relative to other metropolitan areas, the growth continued from 1960 to 1970 based on the vast and diversified tourist and winter visitor industry and the attraction of the area as a prime retirement spot. The largest employer in the county is the Board of Public Instruction, with county government ranked second, Eastern Airlines third, and federal agencies fourth. Among the top twenty employers, only two are manufacturing firms.

When the employment sectors are ranked according to their contributions to total earnings the following ranking emerges—services, wholesale and retail trade, transportation, communications and public utilities, government and manufacturing. A partial explanation for the position of manufacturing, aside from small numbers of workers, is the wage structure of manufacturing which is heavily weighted with low wage industries. From 1960 to 1970 the most notable changes in earnings were in wholesale and retail trade, which declined almost 3 percent. Manufacturing, services, and government all gained about 1 percent. The increases in manufacturing and services were greater in employment than in earnings, contributing still further to an already uneven distribution of earnings. The trade sector experienced a similar shift.

The major concentrations of strip commercial development are found in the central and northern portions of the region, whereas the major shopping center sites are in the CBD, Miami Beach, Coral Gables, and Hialeah. While the past was characterized by unplanned strip commercial development, the more recent trend has been that of centralized, planned shopping centers.

The great bulk of Miami's industrial uses are found in several major industrial strips on the north side of the city (Figure 12). Railroads are responsible for the location of most of these concentrations, for the railroads in Miami preceded industrial development and later afforded access to state and national markets. Other areas developed with the growth of trucking, especially light industry on the major arteries and expressways. Areas near the airport feature a variety of aircraft support services.

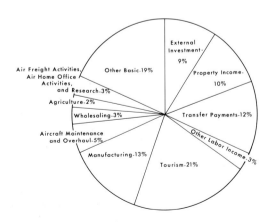

Figure 11. Dade County's 1970 economic base.

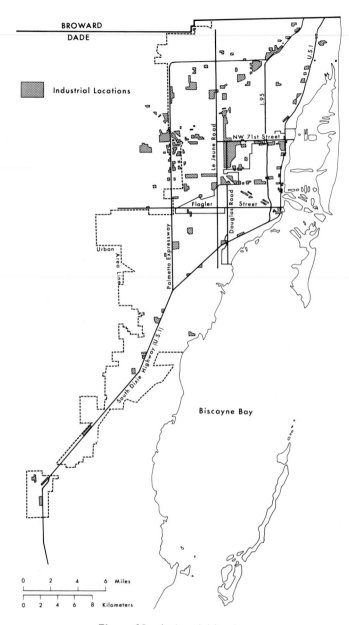

Figure 12. Industrial land uses.

Agricultural activity is concentrated in the southern part of the SMSA, extending from Perrine to Homestead. These areas of rockland and relatively infertile soils produce tomatoes, potatoes, lettuce, celery, and other vegetables. Sunshine is the main resource. Citrus fruits such as limes, mangoes, and avocados are also grown. Between Perrine and Homestead several small communities are strategic shipping points for these row crops.

Housing

In 1972, of the 450,000 housing units in the Miami area, only 9,000 were public or publicly subsidized units. It is conservatively estimated that the waiting list for public housing exceeds 10,000. In 1971 the Dade County Planning Department called for construction of 10,000 low and moderate housing units between 1972 and 1974, but production fell short of the goal because federal funding failed to meet needs. Moreover, 23,000 families live in substandard housing units, a fact that intensifies the problem of low and moderate income housing in Miami. Not surprisingly, black residential areas suffer the most.

In 1960, the vacancy rate for the Miami SMSA was about 7 percent; rapid immigration cut the rate to 3 percent by 1970 despite an average annual rate of construction of about 10,500 units, few of them for low or moderate income households. Multiple family units concentrate in North Dade, Hialeah, Miami Beach, Kendall, and Homestead, whereas single family housing is disproportionately located in South and West Dade and in Carol City. Little construction is taking place in black residential areas, despite some drastic losses from expressway construction. In central Miami alone 3,300 families were displaced or relocated because of highway construction during the late 1960s. Another reason for low overall vacancy rates is the influx of Cuban refugees who tended to locate initially in the lower income housing area radiating westward from the CBD along SW 8th Street.

In 1960, 59 percent of all occupied units were owned, but in 1970 this proportion had dropped to 55 percent as new construction emphasized apartment construction. The abundance of new and expensive rental units has raised average rent levels. Median rent in Miami was $122 per month in 1970, compared to $94 for the state of Florida and $90 nationwide. Home values in Miami are also among the highest in the nation, again reflecting the large proportion of newer units. Miami ranked tenth in 1970 with a median value of $19,000 while the U.S. figure was only $17,000.

There are more than 58,000 overcrowded units in Miami—about 14 percent of the housing stock. Since 1960 there has been a 3 percent increase in overcrowded units while Florida and the nation recorded decreases. Rental units are more prone to overcrowding than owner-occupied ones in Miami. For the most part, apartments, with fewer rooms and a predominance of low income and black and Latin families are the most frequent type of overcrowded multiple family unit. In 1970, the proportion of overcrowded units stood at 18.2 percent for Latin families and 17.7 percent for blacks.

About 5 percent of the total housing stock in Miami is classified as being substandard as indicated by a Dade County Community Improvement Program Blight Survey in 1971. Spatially, the major areas of substandard housing are the Miami core and the Liberty City area between Snake Creek and Bunche Park. About 6 percent of the black-occupied units are substandard compared to 3 percent for Latins.

Poverty

There are fourteen blighted poverty areas in Dade County (Figure 13). Opa Locka, Model City, Central Miami, South Miami, Perrine, Coconut Grove, Goulds-Princeton, and Homestead-Florida City are predominantly black; West Little River and Edison-Little River have a rapidly expanding black population; and Southwest Hialeah, although predominantly Latin, contains a very poor all-black enclave, Seminola. The others are Latin-dominated Little Havana and River North, and the white non-Latin South Beach area.

In all of these areas run-down, overcrowded housing and difficulty in meeting rents and mortgage payments are common. All are above the county average for population density and below average in family income. All areas have sizable percentages below the poverty level, defined in 1970 as $3,743 for a family of four. In most of the areas there are high percentages of children not residing with both parents. Crime and death rates are usually higher than elsewhere in the region, and all have serious environmental problems—standing water on streets, weed-filled vacant lots, uncollected trash, the lack of sewers, lack of open space, and haphazard zoning.

Crime

In 1970 the Miami SMSA had the highest rate of serious crimes (murder, forcible rape, robbery, aggravated assault, burglary, larceny $50 and over in value, and auto theft) of all metropolitan areas within the United States. In 1972 its crime index rate was 5,151 per 100,000 inhabitants, higher than the national average of 2,830 per 100,000 inhabitants, and far ahead of such places as New York, Chicago, and Philadelphia. The central city of Miami reported that its crime index rate for the

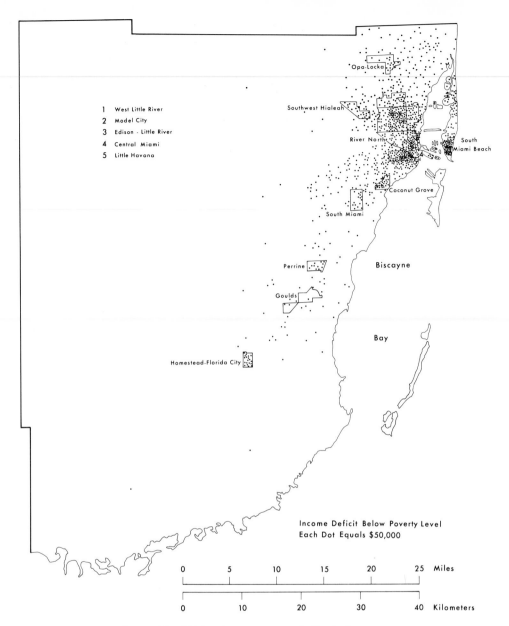

1 West Little River
2 Model City
3 Edison - Little River
4 Central Miami
5 Little Havana

Income Deficit Below Poverty Level
Each Dot Equals $50,000

| 0 | 5 | 10 | 15 | 20 | 25 | Miles |

| 0 | 10 | 20 | 30 | 40 | Kilometers |

Figure 13. Blighted poverty areas in Dade County.

first four months of 1974 had risen more than 18 percent above the rate of reported crimes for the same period in 1973. This increase took place despite a doubling of the number of police officers on the streets.

Two offenses—robbery and murder—are of special significance. For the first four months of 1974, robbery increased 26 percent over the same period for the previous year. Murder increased 10 percent, apparently because of its connection with organized crime. So-called

gangland killings may have contributed significantly to the overall crime rate in recent years. For example, the *Miami Herald* reported that "41 men and women have been found shot, stabbed, bludgeoned, butchered, and burned in gangland slaying in the last eight years." Usually a crime with a high clearance rate, only eight of these forty-one killings have been solved. According to the *Herald*, the biggest concern of law enforcement officials is that increasing law enforcement pressure in northern East Coast cities might drive more organized crime to the South Florida area.

Miami is a city of vibrant contrasts. Each neighborhood displaying its unique combination of social, economic, and ethnic attributes. Some areas remain prosperous and comfortable, yet, as in other cities, certain neighborhoods collect more than their share of the worst problems. It is to Miami's neighborhoods that we next turn our attention.

Neighborhood Characteristics and Urban Structure

Bounded on the east by the coast, urban development is confined to the 180° half circle radiating inland from the Atlantic Ocean. Land-based communication is made difficult by Miami's regional setting at the southern tip of a 450 mile long peninsula. This situation of regional isolation is further compounded by the low-lying Everglades, which almost completely surrounds the remaining land margins of the Miami urban area. Given these physical characteristics of the site, penetration points into Miami are few in number and have had great impact on the developing form and structure of urban Miami.

DEVELOPMENT CORRIDORS

Six development corridors constitute the Miami urban system (Figure 14). Each of the high income sectors is buffered from the low income areas by a middle income corridor. Within the urban setting, these development corridors are made even more functional by physical access limitations created by certain terrain and drainage features which frequently form the boundaries between growth wedges. Although small in scale, there are a number of instances where canals and other lowland development obstacles raised formidable barriers to communication. The existence of such conditions has made it possible for apparently adjoining neighborhoods to evolve independently their own distinctive characteristics in an atmosphere free of the effects of interaction.

Miami Beach

The sandbars which parallel the east coast of Florida and form the coastal beaches are separated from the mainland by saltwater bays and lagoons. That southern portion of the coastal beach which lies within Dade County is Miami Beach, stretching northward from Government Cut some fourteen miles to the Broward County line.

Bounded as it is by the Atlantic Ocean on one side and Biscayne Bay and the Intercoastal Waterway on the other, the peninsula constitutes a natural development corridor. Because of its unique physical character and location and its separation from the mainland, Miami Beach has developed as a distinctive unit within the Miami urban system.

Carl Fisher, John Collins, the Lummus brothers, and others spent millions of dollars preparing the land for development. Their objective was to build a place where, in Fisher's words, "the old could grow young, and the young never grow old." The obstacles were many as hundreds of acres of the beach peninsula were in swamp, a black oozy mire crisscrossed with roots and branches of stiltlike mangrove. The mangroves were chopped down and covered with fill sucked from the bottom of the bay. This filled land was then covered with black dirt from the Everglades and divided into lots, leaving space for polo, golf, and tennis grounds. Lincoln Road, to have been the Rue de la Paix of the western world, now the Lincoln Road Shopping Mall and closed to vehicle traffic, was cut through the jungles to the sea.

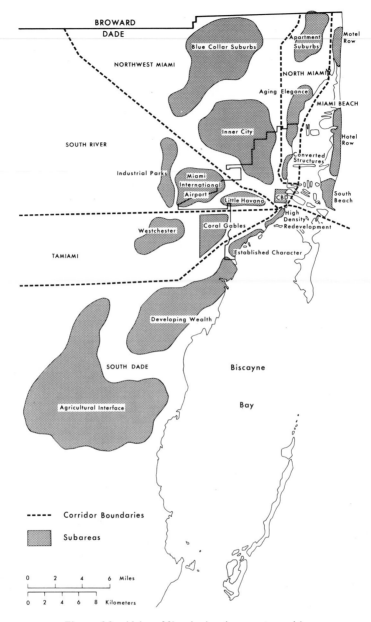

Figure 14. Urban Miami: development corridors.

The town of Miami Beach was incorporated in 1915 following a great publicity campaign which included a varicolored dome on top of the Flamingo Hotel visible for miles at sea, gondolas with native Venetians on the canals, and each day a new galaxy of bathing beauties passing beneath the palms. The beach grew in activity and population so that by the early 1920s it had become the new focal point of Miami's tourism.

Miami Beach has experienced three distinctive development surges during its history of growth. Each of these surges was tourist oriented and each has left a unique imprint upon succeeding beach sections identified respectively as South Beach, Hotel Row, and Motel Row (Figure 14). Given the cyclical nature of many of the urban development and redevelopment processes at work within the urban area, the classic effects of time are clearly discernible in the urban landscape along the beach corridor.

South Beach. Originally a coconut plantation in the early 1900s, South Beach became the initial focal point of tourism on Miami Beach. Developed by the Lummus brothers, its hotels and apartments were generally quite small by current standards of ocean front development (Figure 15). As newer more lavish hotels and apartments were built northward the older South Beach slowly converted from a predominantly transient tourist area to an elderly and predominantly Jewish retirement haven as many persons retired to their

vacationland of earlier days. A virtual geriatric ghetto, 72 percent of the 43,000 South Beach residents are sixty or more years of age. In addition, 47 percent of the area's residents have either Polish or Russian origins, indicating Jewish background.

Located south of Collins Canal, South Beach is almost totally multifamily residential in character with only 3 percent of its dwelling units in single family structures. Dwelling unit density at twenty-six per residential acre is extremely high, but an average population density of forty people per residential acre, although more than three times the country average of 13.1, is not as high as in other parts of urban Miami nor does it cause the problems that might develop were the nature of the area other than that of a retirement community. Had the existing occupany rate of less than 1.7

Figure 15. Low-rise hotels (two to four stories) typical of the older section of South Beach which was the initial focal point of tourism on Miami Beach.

persons per unit been closer to the county average of 2.93 persons per occupied unit, residential densities would exceed seventy persons per acre. As it is, 27 percent of the residential units are overcrowded.

Housing is undoubtedly the worst problem in the area. The average age of structures is high and buildings are crowded together without regard for open space or compatible uses. Rooming houses, movie theaters, hotels, apartments, bars, offices, and retail establishments are found adjacent to each other. While most of South Beach is still in acceptable condition, many of the buildings in the area are deteriorating. This is especially true for the southern portion of the beach where 36 percent of the dwelling units are deficient.

The area's housing stock in its present state has come full cycle, having filtered down to those least able to pay for housing. Average family and unrelated individual income of $6,051 is the lowest of any area in Miami, and over 62 percent of the area's population subsists at less than established poverty levels. In addition, an overwhelming 79 percent of the households pay more than a quarter of their income for housing.

The seriousness of the housing problem has made retirement unpleasant for older people who cannot afford the higher rent for larger housing units in better condition in other parts of the metropolitan area. A trend toward the closing and demolishing of older hotels and structures has already begun. If continued, this trend will soon produce an ever-increasing stream of displaced residents with no place to go.

Buffering South Beach from the results of the second surge of high intensity development is a residential zone of lower density. During the early years dozens of the nation's great industrial leaders and other men of wealth either bought or built palatial homes and estates under the tropic sun in this peripheral zone bordering the initial intensive development core. This small area contains 58 percent of the single family homes built on Miami Beach and is probably the only zone on the beach that could be described as being at least partially single family in nature. Manmade islands, constructed with fill from channel dredging operations, dot the bay side of the beach in this area (Figure 16). Development of these islands has been almost exclusively single fam-

ily residential and though many of these structures are getting old, they add a special air of elegance to this portion of the beach.

Hotel Row. A series of disasters followed the first boom and, while development was far from dormant, hurricanes, the Depression, and World War II greatly reduced development pressures for a number of years. At the end of World War II, Miami Beach was crowded far beyond capacity by friends and relatives of servicemen. New residents, fewer than usual during the hostilities, started making up for lost time, and tourism flourished once again.

It has been said that in the years immediately following World War II, more deluxe hotels were built in the new resort area of Miami Beach than in all the rest of the world. During this period and through the 1950s the great concrete canyon was constructed, running for miles along the ocean side of the beach (Figure 17). Today concrete and cabanas obstruct both the resident's and tourist's view of the ocean. The beach is seldom used as a recreational resource anymore.

In time the character of tourism changed, geared more to the middle income tourist as plastic and tinsel luxury replaced the older luxury for the upper class. Nightclubs abounded and casual hotel visitors left Miami Beach imagining the resort atmosphere to be typical of the entire metropolitan area.

However, the products of this development mode are beginning to suffer the effects of age and change in the tourist industry. Several large hotels have converted to condominiums. If the trend increases, the decline in tourist and convention space would undermine the tourist industry, already under increasing threats from both internal and external sources.

The most concentrated section of hotels typical of the second surge of development is bordered by a zone of lower residential density. This zone, just outside the corporate limits of the city of Miami Beach, is comprised of a number of small incorporated communities including Bay Harbor Island, Surfside, and Bal Harbour. While these communities contain 24 percent single family houses, compared to 14 percent for the beach as a whole, there are fewer here than in the previous lower density buffering zone, reflecting the general trend toward higher intensity utilization of dwindling land resources along the beach.

Figure 16. Geometric shaped manmade islands which dot the bay side of Miami Beach were constructed with fill obtained from the dredging of ship channels in Biscayne Bay.

Motel Row The most recent surge of development has seen the rise of Motel Row. Strung out one after another on the ocean side of the beach, large and frequently ornate motels extend for at least two miles northward from Haulover Beach Park (Figure 18). Begun in the late 1950s and continued into the 1960s with little or no control, the tourist industry has produced a classic specialized strip development. Geared almost exclusively to entertainment and tourist services, the area pulses with nightlife and has, in recent years, become a focal point of local youth culture and a gathering place for vacationing students.

This area also contains the only remaining undeveloped land along Miami Beach. Following the housing market shift to multiple family units in the late 1960s, most of this land is being used for the construction of high density rental and condominium structures. These high-rise structures interspersed by a scattering of motels dominate the bay side of the highway along this section of the beach. The first of these structures were rental apartments but most newer construction produces condominiums. In fact, many rental structures no more than a few years in age have already changed ownership status and are selling as condominiums.

A major theme of these high density residential developments is one of security. In fact, these high-rise buildings might be more appropriately referred to as minifortresses. The emphasis is on personal services and personal security and each in a sense is a little city unto itself offering a wide variety of goods and services.

North Miami

Flagler's railroad, among the earliest transportation arteries to penetrate the Miami area, served as the axis for an urban development

Figure 17. Luxury hotels form the concrete canyon which runs for miles along the ocean side of Miami Beach.

Figure 18. The Castaways Motel in the heart of Motel Row on Miami Beach.

corridor whose apex formed near the entrance to the Venetian Causeway (the first bridge system to link Miami Beach with the mainland), just north of the Miami CBD and the old Miami port facility. The West Dixie Highway followed the railroad in the northern section of the county. Early growth extended rapidly northward along this corridor. Current development is spilling across the county line.

The area is residential in character, with moderate income levels, older residents, and small households. Housing is predominantly single family owner occupied and the structures are of good quality and condition, although somewhat older in age. One of the most stable sections of the city, there has been little opportunity for black or Spanish settlement.

The innermost or oldest portion of North Miami is being transformed, as many older single family homes are converted into multiple unit structures. Beyond this zone of converted dwellings lie several elegant enclaves in which housing refuses to filter down to lower class use. Miami Shores, two and one-half square miles with a population of 9,425 in 1970, is one such study in the maintenance of urban elegance. It was built about six miles north of downtown Miami as a high class residential community and remains prosperous today. Although Miami Shores has not attained the national image enjoyed by the city of Coral Gables, it has been able to maintain an outstanding level of services.

Land development practices of the 1920s typically included fifty foot lots and this is reflected in many of the subdivisions situated within the city limits. However, the Miami Shores zoning ordinance specified seventy-five feet as the minimum frontage. This decision alone has been a dominant influence in the creation and maintenance of the present residential pattern.

Urban development encountered farther out along the North Miami corridor is more typically middle class suburban in character. Toward the development fringe both incomes and multiple unit structures show a dramatic increase (Figure 19). Conforming to current housing trends in Florida, growth at the developing margin features vertical suburbs (Figure 20).

Northwest Miami

Largest of the development corridors, the northwest sector encloses 33 percent of the urbanized land and 39 percent of urban Miami's population. Population density is high. The average household size at 3.3 is larger and younger than other sections. Northwest Miami contains 48 percent of the persons under eighteen, 49 percent of all persons below poverty levels, and 49 percent of Miami's crowded housing units. The housing vacancy rate of 4 percent indicates a tight market and shortage of low income housing. This sector houses 82 percent

of the black population and 40 percent of the Cubans. As one might surmise, average family incomes in this corridor are lower than those for any of the other corridors, falling more than $2,000 below the metropolitan average. In short, Northwest Miami is the low income sector with the worst housing, the most overcrowding, and the city's highest crime levels (Figure 21).

The Miami River, forming the southern boundary of this corridor, extends inland four and one-half miles before becoming the Miami Canal and eventually connecting with Lake Okeechobee seventy-five miles to the north. U.S. 27 parallels the waterway to the east and provided the initial path for growth within the corridor. The canalized river is navigable for less than six miles, yet during hurricane periods it provides refuge for private and commercial watercraft.

Figure 19. The unusual structure which could be equated with the promotional structures of the 1920s is the activities center for the Jade Gardens development.

Figure 20. The 21st century complex which advertises "Everything You Came to Florida For" is representative of the increasingly vertical dimension of urban growth in northern Miami.

Figure 21. Frequently project housing has served only to intensify the negative image of the ghetto and has done very little in the way of alleviating poor living conditions and overcrowding.

Central Business District. Downtown Miami, unlike the CBDs of large cities that developed before the auto era, has never achieved the classical central focus or intensity of vertical development so typical of most other downtown areas (Figure 22). At the same time it is similar to them in many other respects.

In many respects downtown Miami has never been busier than today. Perhaps classier before the shopping center era, but never with more daytime bustle, over 40,000 people work in the CBD bounded by NE 7th Street, the Florida East Coast railroad, the Miami River, and Biscayne Boulevard, up about 8,000 in the last five years. Transit carries 32,100 passengers into the downtown area on an average weekday, up 6 percent in two years. According to one estimate, there are 150 more merchants operating in the CBD now than there were ten years ago. The downtown area offers 14,000,000 square feet of commercial floor space. There are no vacant store fronts along Flagler and other main streets.

However, the downtown's seeming vitality is only a half-life. Like many other cities the CBD has problems as persistent as the setting of the sun and many of them begin about the same time. Downtown thrives by day, but it dies at night. The sodium vapor lights that help police chase away the crime also serve to illuminate the empty streets. People once came to stroll and see others. Honky-tonks lined the streets and crowded sidewalks overflowed into the street. But no more. The nightlife has relocated. Some of the smaller shops have a brisk trade after sunset. They are sustained by a new and undocumented phenomenon in the Miami economy—the shopper from abroad. Touring Latins and islanders are nighttime people in the Spanish tradition. If this new trend is sustained it may revitalize downtown Miami. The U.S. Travel Service estimates that more than a million Latin tourists visited the United States last year, spending more than $1 billion before they left. Florida's share of the Latin vacation extravaganza is more than a third of the total and most of it stays in Miami. Traditionally, Colombians, Central Americans, and Peruvians have been Miami's best customers. But the large developing countries of Brazil, Venezuela, and Argentina are now providing an increasingly large number of tourists.

Inner City. Miami never had a big industrial function but what little industry it had located early at one of two sites. West of the CBD along the Miami River land use is wholly commercial-industrial and includes a large power plant, shipping companies, boat yards, fish houses, a few restaurants, marine supply firms, and other water-oriented businesses.

A second early industrial concentration follows Flagler's Florida East Coast railroad north of the CBD. Initial tenants were replaced by the garment industry, but clothing factories have begun shifting to suburban locations further northwest (Figure 23). The inner city industrial area threatens to become an industrial slum.

One positive element in this area is the Civic Center area. In addition to a number of government buildings and government functions, this area is also the site of the city's major medical complex including Jackson Memorial Hospital, the University of Miami Medical School, Cedars of Lebanon Hospital, the Cerebral Palsy Clinic, the National Cardiac Children's Hospital, and the U.S. Veterans' Administration Hospital.

The inner city is also home for more than 75 percent of northwest Dade's blacks. Concentrated in two neighborhoods, they are expanding and coalescing into one large "black oval" slanting across the interchange of the Airport Expressway and I-95 (Figure 24). Merging of the two ghettos is the result of blacks replacing Latins moving out of the three-quarter mile gap that now separates the Brownsville-Liberty City area from what has long been called the "Central Negro District." Latin neighborhoods are spreading into Hialeah and the Westchester section of West Dade in the Tamiami development corridor. Serious clashes between the races have been minimal in the Miami area, but blacks and Cubans are not inclined to share the same neighborhoods.

Blue Collar Suburbs. One terminal point for the Latin exodus from the inner city debarkation point has been Hialeah. This largest of Miami's incorporated suburbs had 102,000 persons in 1970, 45 percent of them Latin. The new plants and new jobs in the garment industry's shift to the suburbs have concentrated in Hialeah. Spanish-speaking workers form the largest segment of the labor force in the industry. The garment industry more than

Figure 22. The Miamarina and Bayfront Park in the foreground provide the setting for downtown Miami's modest skyline.

Figure 23. Clothing factories in Miami's garment district.

Figure 24. Typical of older housing in the central Miami ghetto, this row of "shotgun shacks" stands across the street from a large neglected tract of land that was razed several years ago.

doubled in size between 1965 and 1970 and is now the largest single element in the industrial labor force with 537 firms employing more than 18,000 workers. Aluminum fabrication is also concentrated in Hialeah, especially in the area along the Seaboard Air Line Railroad, the second of two railroads serving Miami.

Other blue collar suburbs include Opa Locka and Carol City. Opa Locka grew out of an aborted 1920s land boom development. Later it serviced the now inactive Opa Locka Naval Air Station. Today it houses a predominantly low income black community many of whom occupy institutional type housing erected during the period of activity at the naval air station. Carol City is currently Miami's only example of an integrated suburban development.

Interesting to note is the apparent locational anomaly of Miami Lakes, a prestigious, high income community situated directly in the path of Miami's rapidly expanding low income corridor. Miami Lakes began some fifteen years ago as a planned community (new town) situated on about five square miles of former pasture land. When the parcel was first purchased for cattle grazing the owner observed, "It was one of the ugliest pieces of land in Dade County, but it was high ground." The fact is that little high (dry) ground remains and most of it will eventually be converted to high income development regardless of its location. Moreover, this development, like most in Dade County, may be large enough to make its future more dependent on internal features than on external locational considerations.

South River

The South River corridor has a low income character resembling that of the Miami River corridor. Access points across the river separating them are few, as are similarities beyond that of income. Next to Miami Beach, South River has the highest percentage of multiple family dwelling units. As a result, dwelling unit density and population density are high. Overcrowded units are more prevalent in this sector than in any other sector. Indicative of the overcrowding and high demand for housing within this corridor is the low vacancy rate, less than 2.4 percent in 1970.

One element helping to account for the tight housing situation is the Latin population, 61 percent of the corridor total. The majority of these Spanish-speaking residents live in the area known as Little Havana. A second distinctive feature is Miami International Airport. Under the influence of the airport and expressway links, the area west of the airport is developing industrially. Much of the land has been zoned for industrial park development.

It is in Little Havana that the Latin culture first took root in Miami. It is here that one still finds the best restaurants, the largest Latin groceries, the Spanish movies, and the private bilingual schools. It encompasses SW 8th Street and West Flagler as its main center of trade. More than three-fourths of its 70,000 residents are Spanish-Speaking.

Old Havana may well be gone, but new Havana in Miami sparkles with restaurants, nightclubs, and shops. Signs and advertisements are all in Spanish (Figure 25). Hardly a word of English is spoken. Old Havana favorites such as the Floridita, frequented by Ernest Hemingway, the Zaragoyana restaurant next door, and the popular Centro Vasco all have established their Miami counterparts (Figure 26).

The original Zaragoyana, Havana's best seafood restaurant, was established in 1832. Transported to Miami, it has emerged in the form of

Figure 25. Neighborhood shopping center in "Little Havana."

Figure 26. The Centro Vasco Restaurant in the heart of Miami's "Little Havana" area.

two of Miami's most extravagant nightclubs—one Spanish, and called the Flamenco; the other as Cuban as a foot long cigar, Les Violins. About all that is missing from the streets of Little Havana are the cries of the lottery ticket vendors and perhaps the covered arcades.

Drug stores feature *Cosmopolitan en Espanol,* copies of "How to Become a Citizen," and Spanish comic books. Grocery store shelves stock cans of black beans, guava marmalade, green papaya chunks, mango slices, and squid in its ink, imported in tins from Spain. Postcards depict Miami's Little Havana as *La Capital del Exilio* (the capital of the exiles). Others carry pictures of the monument erected to those who fell at the Bay of Pigs, burning with an eternal flame and displaying the names of those who fell.

Little Havana has large concentrations of multifamily housing and some single family residences but renters outnumber owners five to one. Age distribution reflects fewer children and more elderly than respective county rates. As so often happens, this older central area tends to retain the poor, the elderly, the most recent arrivals, and those who for a variety of reasons are less absorbed into the American way of life.

Housing and land use problems are relatively severe in Little Havana. Heavy commercial strip developments encroach on residential areas. Over 15 percent of the dwelling units are deficient and 31 percent of the housing units are overcrowded. Residential density is thirty-three people per acre and going higher as additional housing units are being built. Cuban immigration has brought vitality to the area, but unless physical conditions are improved the benefits may be lost, especially if the area continues its trend toward overcrowding.

West of Little Havana near the edge of the South River corridor lies Miami International Airport. Approximately half of Dade County's 75,000 airline-related employees work at the airport, with the other half scattered around the county. Miami's airport is among the top five in the world in international cargo movements, domestic jet flights per week, and rate of increase in cargo tonnage and passengers carried by airlines. About 1,400 aircraft arrive and depart on an average day. Approximately

75 percent of the passengers moving through the airport are Miami-bound tourists.

There are seven well-established industrial areas and many scattered plants of various sizes in Dade County. The largest tract is an area of 12,000 acres located west of Miami International Airport and between the Palmetto Expressway and the Southwest Dade Turnpike.

Tamiami

Even in the boom days of 1923 when optimism ran high, traveling directly from Fort Myers on the west coast to Miami was unheard of. If a Fort Myers resident suggested going to Miami, it was just assumed he meant traveling by boat to Tampa, then across the state by auto to Daytona Beach, and finally south to Miami. This trip of 545 miles to cover a distance of 144 miles was likely to take two weeks if you hurried. Thus early urban growth in Miami and the oldest parts of the city lie north and south along the coastal ridge and northwest adjacent to the Miami River.

This was the situation until twenty-five men, including two Seminole Indian scouts, were convinced by the Tamiami Trail Association to cut through the roadless, swampy expanse of the Everglades direct from Fort Myers to Miami. The men naively thought the trip, which began April 4, 1923, would take three days. They finished the trip and returned to Miami after seventeen grueling days of hunger, exhaustion, and fever. Their feat led to the construction of the cross state highway which today is U.S. 41. Five years later this road, which was to open up western Dade County and which serves as the northern boundary of the Tamiami development corridor, was finished at a cost of $7 million. Since that time, the Tamiami corridor, with the exception of the city of Coral Gables, has developed as a relatively stable middle income residential area with the second highest percentage of single family homes among the six urban development sectors.

Coral Gables. One of the earliest and most successful planned communities, Coral Gables, located some six miles south and west of downtown Miami, had a 1970 population of over 42,000 and an average 1969 family income of almost $20,000 compared to $11,380 for metropolitan Miami. George Merrick, the initial owner and developer of Coral Gables, conceived of it as "Miami's Master Suburb." Incorporated as a city in 1925, the developer planned for 10,000 people on 5,000 acres, imagining a great community of Spanish castles surrounded by the best of educational and recreational facilities. Disappointed that so few subdivisions in the East and Midwest tried to make their developments harmonize with their surroundings, he adopted a Mediterranean theme, believing that the South Florida environment matched that of the Mediterranean (Figure 27).

Vigorous advertising in national and local daily papers continually announced new projects for Coral Gables. Hurricanes and the Depression terminated several projects, although many major elements of the planned community were completed before the crash, including all major plazas and entrances, the city hall, the Coral Gables Library, the Venetian Pool, and the Tallman Clinic and Hospital.

Investment in property in Coral Gables was protected by strict building restrictions in the form of building codes and zoning that were built into the plan for the city. These rigid restrictions ensured structural strength, climatic comfort, and visual harmony of architectural style and scale, color and landscape. Zoning provided for beautiful residential areas forever protected from the encroachments of businesses.

The intent of the rigidly enforced building code was to produce buildings as permanent as the solid coral rock itself. Applying equally to residences and business buildings, type and design were regulated so that Coral Gables seems an old world city transplanted to a new world setting.

Westchester. Truncation of the Little Havana area in the South River corridor by Miami's International Airport has obstructed the normal growth processes and forced Cuban expansion to jump to noncontiguous areas. In addition to Hialeah, another predominantly Latin suburban location is in the Westchester sector of Dade County west of Coral Gables. The Latin exodus from the coalescing "black oval" in the Miami River corridor is also accelerating the spread of Latin neighborhoods in Hialeah and Westchester.

South Dade

Second largest of the six development corridors in the area, the South Dade corridor includes most of Miami's highest income neighborhoods. Until the opening of the Southwest Dade Turnpike in April 1974, the South Dixie Highway was the only major artery serving all of South Dade and, until the last few years, most of the urban development south of the

Figure 27. This Spanish style church characterizes the architecture reflected by many of the homes and buildings in Coral Gables.

Figure 28. Perhaps the most ornate of all, Viscaya is one of the few great estates that still survives and is operated currently as a historical museum.

Kendall area focused tightly around this access route.

There is a great variety of development in this sector of the urban area which ranges from the residential estates along Biscayne Bay to the migrant labor camps of the Redlands agricultural area. The corridor includes four urban-process-related sequential sections—the oldest section of high density redevelopment, a stable area of established character, a new area of developing wealth, and the agricultural interface.

The bayfront land along Brickell Avenue from the Miami River south several miles to Coconut Grove became a prime residential area starting in the 1920s. While Miami was living off tourism, great estates and ornate mansions flourished along Brickell Avenue and east to Biscayne Bay (Figure 28).

Then as Miami grew and the local economy began to flex its muscles, Brickell Avenue began to change. One by one the old homes came down to make way for office buildings. The Brickell area is now a one mile stretch south from the Miami River and is fast becoming the heart of Miami's booming financial section.

At the heart of the older prestige section of Miami is Coconut Grove, rich in South Florida history. Even before Henry Flagler's railroad chugged this far south and even before there was a Miami, there was a Coconut Grove with people hacking an existence out of the wilderness.

Annexed by the city of Miami in 1925, the Grove—or "the Villages," as it is still affectionately called by residents—has developed into an unorthodox community where the poor rub elbows with the wealthy and the talented. It was not uncommon to find someone from *Who's Who* spending the winter in a wooden bungalow next door to an illiterate.

The narrow preautomobile streets frequently dead-end, segmenting the Grove into secluded residential pockets. Turning off the main highway today a visitor finds tree-lined trails flanked by a mixture of rich estates, modern houses, Spanish villas, English cottages, and perhaps a weather-beaten boards and batten shack next door to a mansion. The community, which today is known for its artists and sidewalk art shows, still retains a village type atmosphere. In general residents prefer pedaling bikes to driving cars.

Also contained within the Coconut Grove area is one of urban Miami's black enclaves.

Most of the predominantly black poverty areas —such as the Central District, Liberty City, Brownsville, Opa Locka, South Miami, Perrine, Goulds, Princeton, Naranja, Homestead, Florida City, and Coconut Grove—all began as ghettos and all were located near areas in need of cheap labor. Coconut Grove is one of the oldest. It began as a small black community near the white settlement that grew up around Coconut Grove Habor where Peacock's Inn launched the Gold Coast hotel industry. When the black community developed, its first residents were Bahamians who worked at the Peacock Inn.

Farther out in the South Dade corridor one soon encounters the area of new and developing wealth. In the Old Cutler area and eastward to Biscayne Bay, recent developments such as Gables Estates, Coral Gables by the Sea, and Old Cutler Bay have sprouted on and between the old estate lands of the previous generation. Average family income is $32,949 and residential structures range from $150,000 to $500,000 and up (Figure 29). One-third to one-half acre lots with direct water access to Biscayne Bay sell for more than $100,000.

Representative of development inland is the Kendall area. Average family income at over $20,000 is almost twice the Dade County average. Land prices literally skyrocketed when development began. In the 1930s, land on what would become Kendall Drive could be bought for $1 an acre. Sections here and to the south were under water as much as six months of the year. Then came progress!

In 1958, Congress approved funds for the Black Creek Canal. In the early 1960s land was selling for about $1,000 an acre. By late 1962 the canal, which officials of the Florida Flood Control District said would "turn the wasteland into fertile farm fields," was finished. But the fertile farm lands were not to hold forth for long.

In March of the same year the state Road Department made the four lane paving of North Kendall Drive a priority project. As the road was built, the price of an acre jumped to $2,000, then to $5,700. Land in the Kendall area soon became the hottest commodity in the real estate market. Today land in the Kendall area, if available, would cost as much as $60,000 an acre.

Still farther south a battle rages between urban and agricultural land uses. Agriculture is Dade County's oldest export activity. Al-

Figure 29. Homes in the old Cutler Bay Estates area with direct water access to Biscayne Bay.

though it has declined in the face of tourism, retirees, and manufacturing, over 1,000 farms on 117,000 acres supported about 2.3 percent of the county's population in 1965. Agricultural mainstays of the economy are winter tomatoes, potatoes, beans, mangoes, limes, and avocados.

Much of the initial urban development in this area was an assemblage of predominantly black communities which formed over the years to house semipermanent resident and migrant agricultural workers. By far the largest of these communities are Perrine, Goulds, and Florida City which sit astride U.S. 1. Princeton and Naranja are enclaves representative of the smaller concentrations of farm workers used in the South Dade fields for over half a century.

Traditionally, Dade County's croplands were located on the high, dry coastal ridge. Small plots of land were farmed by individuals with no large financial resources. In recent years, urban development has come to exert tremendous pressures and is forcing agriculture off the ridge into submarginal land in the Everglades and coastal marshes. Actual urban uses for the land are many years off, but the land is still desirable as soil conditions and elevations are good for urban development. Realtors say this is where the next development has to be as this is 95 percent of the county's available land. The recent opening of the Florida Turnpike has all but assured the investor of profits.

Special Groups, Special Problems

Within metropolitan Miami exist many groups whose members are bound together by race, ethnic or national origin, age, and social and economic activities. This section discusses five of these groups—blacks, Cubans, retirees, Miccosukee Indians, and migrant workers. To some extent each is dominant in a particular locale and makes a unique impact on the cultural landscape.

BLACKS

Metropolitan Miami's 190,000 blacks live mainly in ten residential enclaves scattered throughout the northern and southern parts of the region (Figure 30).

Ex-slaves and freed flaves, fleeing discrimination and bondage, sought refuge from the plantation system or other southern states by living among the Seminole Indians of northern and southern Florida. Many intermarried and enjoyed comfortable lives free from racism until the coming of the whites. The Bahamas and the Caribbean Islands have also been source areas for black inmigrants coming for economic reasons.

Coconut Grove was probably the first black settlement in the Miami area. Bahamian blacks constituted the major source of laborers during the later part of the nineteenth century, before Flagler's railroad and the founding of Miami. Accustomed to using the coral rock found in the Bahamas, they brought their masonry skills with them to Maimi. Working without cement, these black Bahamians, with their knowledge of coral and limestone construction, built walls, roads, homes, and larger structures using only native lime mortar. They also brought their knowledge of tropical trees, replacing many of the fruits and vegetables that had been brought by white Bahamians (Conchs) with the pigeon pea, soursop, star apple, sugar apple, Jamaica apples, together with the caneps, sapotas, and dillies of the black Bahamian culture.

After Flagler's railroad reached Miami in 1896, the area to the west of it in central Miami was designated as a residential tract for blacks who worked for the railroad. This Central District became Miami's second black ghetto, containing most of the black population until the 1960s, when the Brownsville and Liberty City areas coalesced to replace it as the largest black residential cluster.

What is it like if you are black and living in the core area of the Miami SMSA? First, you are probably one of the Central District's 21,000 or Brownsville-Liberty City's 88,000 inhabitants. If you live in the former there is a 33 percent chance that your family income falls below the poverty level; if you live in the latter the chance is 22 percent.

A trip through the areas reveals a number of things about poverty that have not been measured. In both the Central District, where "shotgun" housing still exists despite efforts to replace the older style housing with multiple family dwellings, and the Brownsville-Liberty City area, where a Model Cities program attempted to eradicate deplorable physical and economic conditions, residents display am-

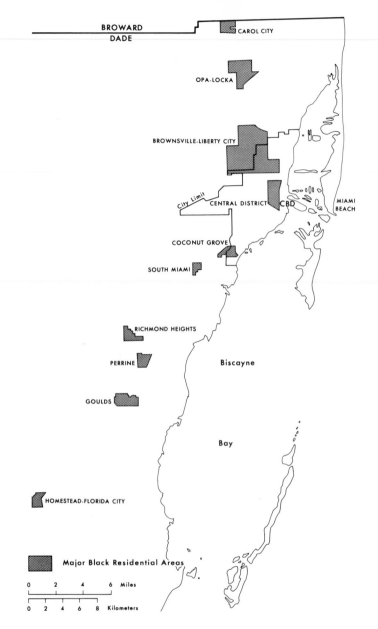

Figure 30. Major black residential areas in metropolitan Miami.

bivalence toward their plight. The existence of their conflicting feelings on one hand comes from black pride and the opportunity to interact with similar persons. On the other hand their unhappiness stems from the failure of society to adjust to the needs of black and poor persons. They attribute their plight to racial discrimination. They simply cannot understand why their housing units are not as

sound as the nonblack ones, and cannot comprehend why Cubans, who have been in Miami a much shorter period of time, have a median family income that is almost $2,600 more than their median income.

The inner ring includes five predominantly black clusters—Coconut Grove, South Miami (or Lee Park), Opa Locka, Richmond Heights, and Carol City. Black communities beyond the margin of the central city partly indicate the desire of blacks to suburbanize. Carol City, Richmond Heights, and Opa Locka are relatively recent developments containing young inmigrants who formerly lived in the core. Coconut Grove and Lee Park are much older communities with many elderly persons.

With the exception of Coconut Grove and Lee Park, the black middle class can be found within the inner ring. Carol City, Richmond Heights, and Opa Locka (Bunche Park), respectively, have the highest median family incomes of all the black communities in the SMSA and also contain a better quality of housing. However, considering the fact that the best for blacks in Miami does not equal the average for the whole of the area, the concept of "black middle class" is somewhat misleading. For example, there are many families where every member of working age must have a job to maintain the family's present status; and in many instances, the head of the household or the major supporter must work around the clock, having a full time job and a part time one, two full time jobs, and in some instances as many as three jobs.

The black communities of Perrine, Goulds (including Naranja and Princeton), and Homestead-Florida City are situated in a semirural setting and are occupied by a less affluent group than either the core or the inner ring. While the core depends to a great extent on the central city for employment, and the inner ring somewhat less so, most of the black residents of the outer ring depend on agriculture for livelihood. The inner ring boasts the highest level of educational attainment; the outer ring the lowest. The housing quality is poorer in absolute numbers in the core, but the outer ring contains the greatest proportion of low housing quality.

Located more than twenty miles from the CBD, many of the residents live in labor camps and constitute a signficant fraction of the permanent agricultural laborers. Even though social and economic conditions are proportionally worse in the outer ring, the small number of black persons affected makes its problems less urgent than those of the core.

All is not bleak for Miami's black residents. Many are engaged in business in Brownsville-Liberty City and elsewhere. Black businesses increased 30 percent from 1969 to 1972, but most are small, grossing less than $100,000

yearly. Black business suffers in that the black community in general has a high unemployment rate that reduces purchasing power; has sent many of its highly trained blacks to white corporations; has many crimes that cause higher insurance rates; has been subjected to credit discrimination; and is much smaller in size than the Cuban and white communities. Even though all is not bleak, the dark side of the black man's existence in Miami overshadows the bright one.

CUBANS

Early in the 1960s the Cuban trickle to the U.S. exploded into a torrent. The federal government embarked on a program to resettle Cuban refugees outside of Miami. Many refugees did settle in other states, but through the years they have returned to Miami in increasing numbers. They often return with substantial savings after just a few years working elsewhere. They settle and establish businesses in Miami for several reasons—relatives, friends, and other persons of similar background; Spanish radio stations, newspapers, and special English-speaking programs; the duplication of Cuban economic and social lifestyles experienced; natural amenities that are similar to those of Cuba; and finally, sheer proximity to the Cuban homeland.

Miami today is truly a bilingual city, with the Cuban population in Dade County as high as 350,000 or almost 30 percent of the population. Of the 83,000 existing Cuban households in Miami, approximatley 88 percent use Spanish at home, even though parents or children may be fluent in English away from home. The typical Cuban emerges as an individual who lives in a family of four, has a year of college, and owns a color television, at least one car, and his own home.

Almost 45,000 Cubans have become American citizens, placing the community in a potentially powerful political position. If the trend toward citizenship continues and the Spanish-speaking population becomes interested in developing the political clout that goes with voting citizenship, they will become a major political force in Dade County by the 1980s.

In their new setting, Cubans follow the American immigrant tradition as industrious, aggressive, and goal oriented. Their impact on Dade's economy has been phenomenal.

Consigned at first to menial jobs, Cubans soon recovered from the shock of relocation. They learned new trades, often working at two or more jobs. They started 7,000 new businesses through loans obtained from various sources with the result that almost one-third of the businesses in Miami are Cuban owned and operated. These range from million dollar firms listed on the stock exchange to one man or family-operated businesses.

Perhaps the greatest effect of the Cubans has been in the booming construction and real estate market. Sixty-two percent of all licensed contractors are Cuban and over 40 percent of all new construction in Miami is done by or for Cubans. Construction projects range from the tallest buildings in downtown Miami to remodeling and rebuilding of old neighborhoods and the initiating of new ones.

Eighty-five percent of the clothing industry's factory operation is composed of Cuban labor, 95 percent of whom are women. The Suave Shoe Corporation is one of the largest of the Cuban-owned businesses in Miami, employing 3,000 people. There are also smaller boutiques of private designers, seamstresses, and women who embroider wedding dresses.

The medical and hospital situation, rather than becoming a problem for the area, has actually been alleviated by doctors who resettled in the area. Approximately 1,200 have passed their boards and have established local practices. Another 2,200 doctors are in the process of revalidating their boards in order to practice. Fifteen outpatient clinics are already in operation. Cuban dentists and attorneys have not been as fortunate as the doctors, and many have been forced to find work in other capacities.

Tobacco is another Cuban industry of importance in Miami (Figure 31). Over twenty cigar factories operate, employing some 300 workers. Fishing, too, has been heavily invaded by Cubans. A large number of fishing vessels are owned and operated by them and provide a large amount of seafood for the local area as well as for markets in other states. Approximately 70 percent of the service stations in the area are owned or operated by Cubans. Hotels are almost entirely Cuban staffed and Cubans represent almost 65 percent of all construction workers.

Spanish restaurants and nightspots number in the hundreds in the Miami area. Whether Cuban and nostalgic, Spanish and dazzling, or cozy and personal with a rhythmic Latin beat, Miami offers all three. Spanish food is served with a gaiety and excitement reflected in the Cuban night life, plus a musical repertoire and history carefully preserved from the homeland.

Other Cuban activities include publication of thirty-nine Spanish-language newspapers and magazines; three television stations broadcasting in Spanish, one full time and the others part time; four full time radio stations; and five theaters which show only Spanish films or American movies with Spanish subtitles. Over twenty-five Cuban-operated private schools are functioning in the Miami area and many more are in the process of applying for the accreditation necessary for admittance to universities.

Politically, the Miami Cuban is a conservative Republican. His voting clout has not yet been fully realized because many are not citizens. In the future their numbers will play larger political roles.

So far the Cubans have a sweet and sour feeling about being away from their homeland, even though almost all of them feel completely at home in Miami. An overwhelming 97 percent of the Cubans surveyed said they had been accepted by Miamians into a life free of resentment and discrimination. Nevertheless, 62 percent said they were less satisfied with their lives today than they were when they lived in Cuba before Castro.

At the same time 40 percent doubted that they would ever get a chance to return to Cuba, and more than fifteen years of Castro government has begun to take its toll. Many are now citizens, and nearly half expect to become citizens. If a political change occurred in Cuba they would like to return to see what has happened, but would not return there to live permanently. Their children are American and increasingly their roots are in Miami.

RETIREES

There were about 146,000 retirees living in the area in 1970, the largest share from the Northeast. Amounting to 12 percent of the total population, most of the older citizens in Dade County reside in the southern part of Miami Beach. Other major concentrations are found in the cities of Miami and Coral Gables and

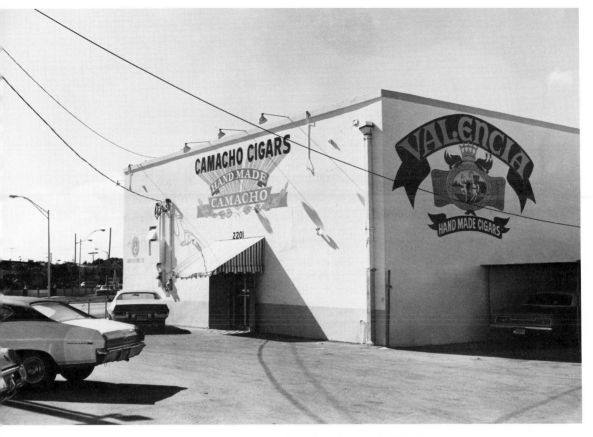

Figure 31. A typical Cuban cigar factory in Miami.

northward along Biscayne Bay in the older communities between I-95 and the bay. From 1960 to 1970 the total retiree population increased 91 percent. Considering that the total population only increased 36 percent, one wonders whether this rapid rate of growth of the older population will continue. Better pension plans and a highly attractive region as a place to live suggest that it will—despite inflation, higher rents and mortgage interest, and the inability of governments to deliver essential services.

Major problems for the retirees in Dade County are income, health, housing, and social well-being. Even though there are various programs in all of these areas, such as the Integrated Nutrition and Social Services to Elderly Persons (better known as IN-STEP), only a small percentage of the elderly needing help are reached. Many fail to receive the medical aid to which they are entitled because of inadequate transportation. What is needed is a better bus system to reach doctors offices, places with meal programs, and recreational facilities designed with the elderly in mind.

In Miami as elsewhere a serious problem for retirees is that of poverty. Housing is a related area of concern. There are about 3,000 units for the elderly which house about 5,000 of the county's 50,000 poor over sixty-five. Almost 15,000 persons are on public housing waiting lists, and over 3,000 of these are elderly. Their plight is worsened in South Miami Beach by the displacement of old hotels and apartments with luxury condominiums.

Miami's elderly are not all sick, conservative in political preference, alienated, physically separated from their children, or dependent. With the exception of a tendency to suffer from certain chronic illnesses, their needs are very much like the remainder of the society.

Southern Miami Beach is a unique situation. Even though the retirees there have many of the problems of the elderly in general, they probably engage in more social interaction than elderly anywhere else in Miami. It is not unusual to pass by one of the theatres or other social activities and see long lines of retirees waiting to enter. It is also not unusual to see many of them sitting on the porches of the old hotels engaging in conversation or playing checkers or cards. South Miami Beach retirees depend upon and interact with one another in many ways.

TOURISTS: NICE PEOPLE

A traditional focal point of the Dade County economy has been tourism. Aside from transfer payments such as pensions and social security, tourism makes the largest single contribution to the economic base of the area, about $448 million from 4.5 to five million tourists in 1970. Lodging and retail establishments each account for over a fourth of this total. Airline operations account for almost a fifth.

The typical tourist flies or drives to the area for a short vacation of approximately one week, and spends and tips conservatively. There are two favorite times of the year. The first is the winter season, which peaks around February, and the second is the summer season. The winter tourist is usually more affluent than the summer one taking advantage of lower rates. A typical winter tourist flies into Miami from the northeastern section of the country, while the summer tourists tend to come from the southeast and arrive by car.

During the last ten to fifteen years there has been a higher percentage of repeat visitors than there was in the past. The average tourist is getting older, indicating that the younger set is going elsewhere for vacations. Perhaps due to fuel costs, more people are leaving their cars at home and flying in, preferring to rent a car if needed. People are staying longer, probably as a result of greater affluence and the time saved in traveling by air.

Most tourists stay in three major locations—the oceanfront of Miami Beach, Surfside, and Bal Harbour. It is in these areas along Collins Avenue that one finds one of the largest hotel and motel rows in the world, catering to the visitor who has come to enjoy a brief stay in the sunshine. Over the years, Miami developed a rather callous attitude toward its transient tourist population that is already reflected in declining tourist dollars. The Miami Beach

Tourist Development Association has launched a campaign to stem the erosion of friendliness and service on Miami Beach. The campaign slogan "Tourists are Nice People" is aimed at reeducating Miamians to the economic importance of tourism.

MICCOSUKEE INDIANS

In the early 1500s, the Creek Nation was composed of two major language groups—Muskogee and Hitchiti. The Hitchiti group was given the name Mikasuki, which eventually evolved to Miccosukee. The tribe occupied parts of the Carolinas and Georgia until the arrival of white settlers in the late 1500s when they began moving inland and southward, settling in northern Florida around Tallahassee. Pressures of colonization in the north, plus armed conflicts, forced the Miccosukee and other of the Creek Nation, known collectively as the Seminoles, to move farther and farther south and eventually into the Everglades where they were able to live in safety. Battles fought in the swamp usually meant Indian victories.

For years, the Miccosukee and other Seminoles roamed Florida, hunting and fishing in the Everglades and farming on the hummocks. But once again, the Indian Removal Act—aimed at the forced relocation of Indians to land west of the Mississippi—caused the Miccosukee to move still farther south to escape forced transfer to Oklahoma. Renewed hostilities broke out and the army drove the Indians farther into the swamps, burning homes and crops in an effort to discourage the Indians and to acquire their much coveted land. Bitter resistance resulted in the Seminole wars. Defeated tribes were resettled on reservations in Oklahoma. The remaining Miccosukee and Seminoles fled into the depths of the Everglades. Living on hummocks and subsisting by fishing and hunting, the Miccosukee successfully adapted to yet another new environment.

With the establishment of the Everglades National Park, the Florida Fresh Water Fish and Game Commission, and various private development projects, more and more land has been taken away from the Miccosukee by state and federal legislation. When the boundaries of the park were expanded northward to their present position, encompassing most of the Indian Hummocks, the Miccosukee were forced to move yet again. Faced with the option of moving to a newly granted state reservation fifty miles to the north that was 90 percent under water and without access roads or development of any kind, or living along a strip of park land in the vicinity of their old hummocks on a use permit basis, they chose the latter. Split off from the larger Seminole tribe that now resides on three reservations ranging from the suburbs of southern Broward County (Hollywood) to the ranch country of central Florida (Brighton) and the relative wilds of the Big Cypress Swamp, the 430 or so Miccosukee live along a five and a half mile long, 500 foot wide strip of land on U.S. 41 (Tamiami Trail) granted them for fifty years by the Bureau of Indian Affairs (BIA). It is here that the Miccosukee, Florida's most traditional and conservative Indians, are making what Tribal Chairman Buffalo Tiger says amounts to their last stand.

Here, in this 350 acre strip of land, the Miccosukee live in their "chickees" (open huts with thickly thatched palm frond roofs), which are inordinately better adapted to the climate and environment of the Everglades than the wood-frame houses the government has attempted to lure them into (Figure 32). It is a simple culture, which even in the day of radio and television counts 80 percent of its numbers as worshippers of the Breathmaker and has its people go deep into the swamp each year for the week long purification ritual of the Green Corn Dance. In the era of equal opportunity it is a clan system in which the ancestry of one's mother influences the role a person will play in tribal affairs.

In the move to their new location along the Tamiami Trail, the Miccosukee were compelled to surrender their self-sufficiency and to change their economic base to the dollar economy. But the adjustment of working for money has

Figure 32. "Chickees" in a Miccosukee village near the Tamiami Trail.

Figure 33. One of the Miccosukee Indian tourist attractions is this exhibition of alligator wrestling.

been difficult for the Indian. Among the last tribes in the nation to accept the paternalism of the Bureau of Indian Affairs, the Miccosukee reluctantly recognized the necessity of mastering this new change in situation to survive. Since 1962 the tribe has been working closely with county, state, and federal agencies

to achieve self-sufficiency once again. According to Buffalo Tiger, the goal is to survive as a Miccosukee tribe and become independent. But as long as they are forced to accept government aid such independence will be elusive.

To end their dependence upon the federal government, the Miccosukee must develop enterprises at which they can succeed, including crafts in which they were highly skilled in the past. Currently, the tribe operates a restaurant, a gas station, and a grocery store and has plans for additional facilities. Tribal members are also employed in education programs for cooking, maintenance activities, administration and planning, and construction related to tribal enterprises. Today, the tribal corporation employs forty-eight Indians and eleven non-Indians, none of whom is responsible to BIA.

Tribal income—derived from their enterprises and a few small pieces of land for which they receive rent—is used to support education and development programs and for financial assistance to tribal members. But according to a 1973 Community Action Program report, 95 percent of the people are still below federal poverty guidelines and the unemployment rate runs 35 percent. Approximately 50 percent of eligible students attend elementary school and only 7 percent attend high school.

Privately, the Miccosukee are engaged in the construction of "chickees," wrestling alligators (Figure 33), managing gift shops, making and selling hand-crafted objects, selling frogs legs, driving air boats, and selling bait and tackle. Occasionally they seek employment in Miami, primarily in construction work. All this, of course, is taking its toll on the traditional Indian way of life (Figure 34). An increasing orientation to the dollar carries with it the potential for wiping out the tribal goal of cultural independence.

MIGRANT LABORERS

At the peak of the winter season (November to mid-April), approximately 8,000 migrant farm

Figure 34. Many of the Miccosukee still prepare food in the traditional manner shown by this Indian woman.

workers, mostly Mexican-Americans and blacks, are found living in about nine "campesinas" strung along U.S. 1 in the southern part of Dade County (Figure 35). About half of these workers live in the area year round. In February 1973 a typhoid epidemic struck the South Dade Labor Camp—the largest of the nine camps. Even though there were no deaths, 218 victims became ill and needed some type of medical attention. The cost of alleviating the problem exceeded $850,000. This epidemic brought attention to the problems of health, sanitation, and overcrowding. Little has yet been done to eliminate the rats, seeping sew-

age, inadequate water supply, and filth. Even though special health projects, the replacement of condemned camps with new trailers, and the creation of various resident organizations have aimed at rectification, more federal, state, and local governmental concern and cooperation must occur before the migrant's environment becomes bearable.

The epidemic in the South Dade Labor Camp is just a symptom of the migrants' condition. People fear for their children's wellbeing. Migrant leaders blame camp owners and health officials for the persistence of the problems; government workers blame the camp

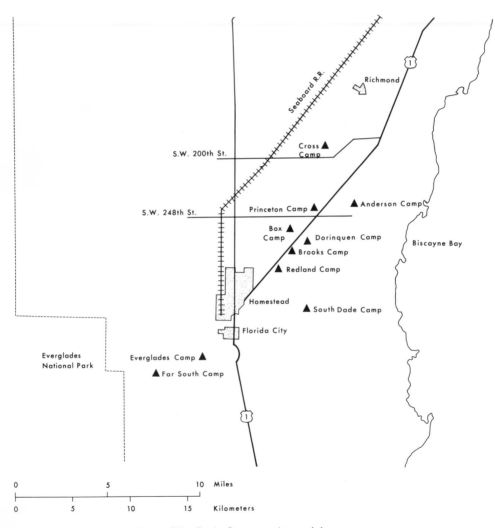

Figure 35. Dade County migrant labor camps.

owners, the migrant workers, and other government agencies. The latter claim that there are about a dozen separate health projects in Florida but none focusing on the migrants. The state Health Department describes the coordination of governmental projects as confused, complicated, cumbersome, and inefficient.

As methods of farming change, old patterns established in the 1920s, when migrants left in late spring or early summer to follow the harvests through the southern states to the northern ones, have also changed. Workers increasingly remain in South Florida as permanent agricultural workers rather than moving about as migrants. Mechanization is one major reason for the increasing number of workers remaining in the area year round. Another is that growing seasons for beans, peppers, potatoes, celery, tomatoes, corn, strawberries, and radishes are much longer, enabling workers to remain in the area almost the entire year.

The problems of the migrant farm workers are aggravated by the low wages and the sometimes inhumane treatment by crew bosses. Wages will probably increase following the activation of a local branch of the United Farm Workers Union because the crew boss, who makes a percentage of what each worker makes, will be replaced by a centralized hiring hall. However, at present the workers are paid an average of about $2.10 per hour for approximately two to three hours per day. Those who do not work by the hour are paid according to the number of buckets of tomatoes, beans, and so forth they pick; the average healthy farm worker can pick from fifty to one hundred buckets per day at a rate of 25 to 30 cents per bucket.

Today and Tomorrow

For years, people have labored under the widely held belief that progress was inexorably linked with growth. In Miami this growth occurred with the blessing and encouragement of civic and governmental leaders. Nationwide campaigns, financed with local tax dollars, sought to attract residents, tourists, and industries to Dade County. The factors that made Miami an attractive subtropical resort for visitors prior to the end of World War II soon attracted thousands of permanent residents, causing one of the highest growth rates for any major metropolitan area.

As Miami grew, it experienced the same general problems as the more heavily industrialized cities of the nation. Citizens now have second thoughts as they witness soaring public service costs, the disappearance of green trees and open fields, water shortages, and a dearth of open beaches and clean water. The fragile ecosystems of southeast Florida cannot withstand alterations. Minimizing the adverse effects on the environment will require sound coordinated planning by developers, governmental agencies, and the public. Preservation of the local environment must be considered synonymous with the preservation of the South Florida economy as the subtropical environment is one of the principal attractions supporting the area's economic base.

PROBLEM AREAS

Hotel Conversions. In the conflict between hotels and condominiums, the hotels in Miami Beach may be losing the battle (Figure 36). If so, the famous Miami Beach sun may soon set on the glittering hotel Gold Coast of yesteryear and Miami Beach may eventually find itself with a shortage of traditional tourist and convention space. The demand for condominium units on Miami Beach is increasing as more old people decide to settle there; in addition, a condominium yields more profit with fewer headaches than a hotel room requiring persistent promotion and service. Currently, further inducements to the trend of condominium conversions on Miami Beach are the limited supply of land on which to build apartment buildings and the constantly increasing cost of construction.

A second reason for the decline in hotels is that older, permanently retired people have been moving into the city of Miami Beach with the result that the city has become less tourist-oriented. Actually, a conflict of interest has arisen between the permanent residents and hotel operators. The type of recreation and entertainment facilities needed by the hotels to lure tourists are of little interest to the long term apartment and condominium dwellers. As time goes by, it is the politics and preferences of more permanent residents that will dominate Miami Beach.

Geriatric Ghetto. Clustered in the South Beach area are Miami's poorest retired persons. Severely afflicted by inflation's insidious attack on their fixed incomes, their haven itself is now being threatened by high-rise redevelopment.

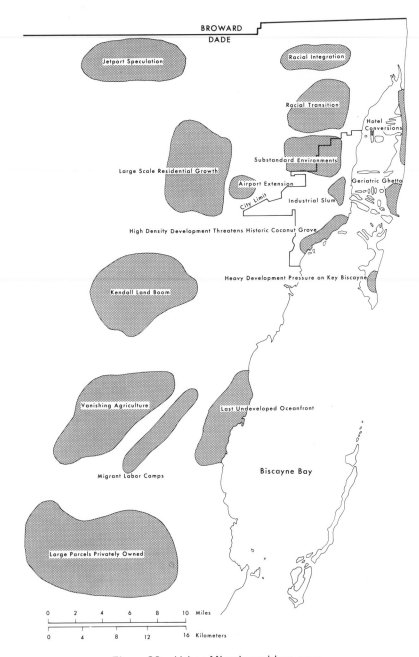

Figure 36. Urban Miami: problem areas.

Heavy Development Pressure. Long a pleasant and sleepy community, Key Biscayne has been rudely awakened by intense development pressures in the last ten years. The site of truly outstanding recreational facilities, access to the key is provided by a single causeway with frequent bridge openings and is already the scene of repeated weekend traffic jams that on occasion exceed weekday rush hour back-ups both in intensity and duration. Key Biscayne is also subject to total inundation during hurricanes and can ill afford excessive high density residential development. Residents resist development proposals in the courts, but numerous high-rise structures already scar the landscape, and the prospect for control is not encouraging.

Threatened Character. High density development has already crept southward along Brickell Avenue and raised its head in downtown Coconut Grove. Expansion and coalescence of these two nodes would destroy the house and residential character of Miami's historical Coconut Grove section.

Undeveloped Oceanfront. The last open oceanfront in urban Miami is located in South Dade and under strong development pressure. Typical of this development pressure is the controversial planned community of Saga Bay, initially planned to house 250,000 people. Conservationists forcefully denounced the planned density and expressed fears over destruction of biologically precious mangroves along Saga Bay's two mile stretch of Biscayne Bay frontage. Debate over the pattern Saga Bay would establish for future developments along the South Dade bayfront resulted in a much modified plan approved by Metro commissioners in 1970. Scaled down plans call for a maximum of 22,053 residential units built over a ten year period.

Migrant Labor Camps. The farm worker in Florida and Dade County has achieved much compared to the conditions CBS film crews documented in shooting "Harvest of Shame" in 1960. But there is still a long way to go, as testified to by the typhoid epidemic and recurring accusations of involuntary servitude in South Dade labor camps.

Land Ownership Problems. Large tracts of land are held in single ownership—for example by U.S. Steel. This situation is conducive to large scale development, and the recent opening of the Homestead extension of the Florida Turnpike has provided accessibility. Speculation and development pressure is now rampant.

Vanishing Agriculture. The Redlands area constitutes one of our nation's prime agricultural resources. But in recent years urban development has relentlessly advanced, spreading unchecked over fertile agricultural soils. Agriculture in turn, with its mechanical pulverizers converting rocky limestone into soil, has been forced to encroach into the agriculturally submarginal and biologically delicate environment of the Everglades. Already South Florida's winter tomato industry has begun to relocate in Mexico.

Kendall Land Boom. When Kendall Drive's four lanes first penetrated underdeveloped land for more than eight miles into the middle of nowhere it triggered a land boom almost without precedent. Projects in progress or on the boards exceed proposed densities for the area by more than threefold. The pace of growth far outstrips the county's plan for installation of services.

Airport Extension. Plans to extend Miami International Airport west to the Palmetto Expressway will likely create serious conflicts with existing and newly developing residential areas.

Large Scale Development. In the area of the Palmetto Expressway and north of the Tamiami Trail, ownership of land in large tracts is generating large scale development, exemplified by Doral Park and Fountainblue Park. Many schools in northwest Dade are already overcrowded, requiring split shifts and the use of portable classrooms. Response time of emergency and fire vehicles is well above acceptable limits and the five year transportation work program for Dade County does not include roadway improvements necessary to handle additional traffic in the area. Moreover, the southern portion of this area will be directly impacted by the programmed extension of Miami International Airport.

This is also a major aquifer recharge area, and studies by the U.S. Army Corps of Engineers indicate that the hydrologic characteristics of the area are unsuitable for development in the absence of a massive and complex regional land and water control system requiring considerable public investment, which is not anticipated. Large scale urbanization of this area would disrupt hydrologic systems and jeopardize the quality of both surface and ground waters.

Jetport Speculation. "To be or not to be"—that is the question, and the off-again, on-again issue of a jetport in Dade County continues. Following a series of studies spanning several years, several site changes, and a considerable amount of controversy, a seemingly final site has been chosen in northwest Dade County along the Broward county line. Selection of this site has touched off a spiral of land speculation in the area which has only just begun.

Racial Integration. Carol City is the only area in metropolitan Miami where one might say integration is taking place. Efforts at integration are painfully slow and the current situation may prove to be but one more example of a temporary interlude in the typical process of neighborhood succession from white to black.

Racial Transition. Elsewhere the process of neighborhood transition from white to black progresses unabated by attempts to establish an integrated residential environment. Numerous conflicts and confrontations are likely and problems are increasing.

Substandard Environment. Model City is probably the one major area in Miami where the broadest spectrum of urban problems can be found together with the greatest degree of concentration and intensity. While predominantly single family residential, this area contains a variety of other land uses which lack adequate buffer zones. None of this was planned with any regard for the residential character of the area, with the result that land use conflicts are extensive.

Industrial Slum. This area probably contains the severest land use problem in urban Miami. Predominantly multifamily residential, substantial amounts of industrial and commercial development are spread throughout. In fact, some residential areas are completely surrounded by industrial activities. Streets are lined on both sides with parked cars and trucks. During the morning and evening rush hours, traffic congestion with its noise, odors, and dust pollutes the residential neighborhoods. As jobs continue to move out to more suburban areas, additional industrial properties are becoming slums. Deterioration is spilling over neighborhood borders faster than it can be treated.

PROSPECTS

If one projected current trends, metropolitan Miami will continue to bloat and sprawl over the landscape, adding at least one million more people by 1990 on half again as much developed land. Continuation of the present growth pattern would push the limits of urban development farther west and south with a little expansion to the northwest. The specter of an energy crisis, with its implicit need to live closer to work, and pressure from environmentalists to preserve lands to the west of urban Miami as aquifer recharge areas, might prevent growth from reaching the Everglades.

As the urban form of Miami approaches maturity, industrial developments and additional employment centers will punctuate suburbia. Currently, principal employment generators are centered around Miami International Airport, the Civic Center, downtown Miami, Miami Beach, the garment district, Hialeah, the area west of the airport, and other smaller areas around the Golden Glades Interchange, Homestead, and the new civic center in South Dade.

Tourism—which is already waning—is likely to continue its decline as the urban system of Miami in growing larger is losing some of its unique character as a tourist attraction. Taking its place will be office, financial, and research growth compatible with the economic base and environment of the area and complemented by Miami's international transportation support system. Medical and higher educational activities are also likely to increase as Miami solidifies its growing role as an international gateway to Latin America.

On the bleaker side, agricultural land is disappearing from the southwest section of the country, and available recreational land is becoming more scarce. Already the finger glades in the southeast section of the county in the Old Cutler Road area are being filled in and the opportunity for intermittent green belts lost. The only respite from urban development is the open space that remains on the urban perimeter. Hopefully some of it can be saved. The decade of the 1970s will probably represent a turning point in the future of urban Miami. The issue is whether Miami shall emerge from the 1970s in sunshine or shadows. Without effective land use and water resource planning, enforcement of pollution abatement, and responsible actions on the part of the government and citizens, the future may fall short of the potential of this magnificent place.

At one point in *Alice in Wonderland,* Alice questions the Cheshire Cat: "Would you tell me, please, which way I ought to go from here?" and the cat responds: "That depends a great deal on where you want to get to." The cat has delineated precisely the issue at hand in Miami.

Bibliography

Berry, Brian J.L. "Internal Structure of the City." *Law and Contemporary Problems* 30 (1965): 115.

Burgess, Ernest W. *"Growth of the City."* In Robert E. Park, Ernest W. Burgess, and Roderick D. Mckenzie, eds., *The City.* Chicago: The University of Chicago Press, 1925.

Churchill, Henry S. *The City Is The People.* New York: Reynal and Hitchcock, 1945.

Dade County Port Authority. *Annual Report.* Miami, 1970.

Fox, Karl A., and Kumar, Krishna T. "Delineating Functional Economic Areas for Development Programs." Mimeographed. Ames, Iowa, 1964.

Friedmann, John. "Two Concepts of Urbanization: A Comment." *Urban Affairs Quarterly* 1, 4 (June 1966): 78-84.

Harris, C.D., Ullman, E.L. "The Nature of Cities." *The Annals of the American Academy of Political and Social Science* 242 (November 1945): 7-17.

Hoyt, Homer. *The Structure and Growth of Residential Neighborhoods in American Cities.* Washington, D.C.: United States Federal Housing Administration, 1939.

"The Industry Capitalism Forgot." *Fortune Magazine,* August 1947.

Jenna, William. *Metropolitan Miami: A Demographic Overview.* Coral Gables: University of Miami Press, 1972.

Lotz, A., and Wood, Thomas J. "Dade County Florida." Working paper prepared February 21, 1974 for RANN Research Project, University of Miami, Center for Urban and Regional Studies.

Marks, Henry S. "Earliest Land Grants in the Miami Area." *Tequesta* (Historical Association of Southern Florida) 18 (1958): 15-21.

Marshall, Arthur R. "South Florida: A Case Study in Carrying Capacity." Paper delivered at the annual meeting of the American Association for the Advancement of Science, 1972.

Merrick, George E. "Pre-Flagler Influences on the Lower Florida East Coast." *Tequesta* 1, 1 (March 1941): 1-10.

Metropolitan Dade County Community Improvement Program. *Profile of Metropolitan Dade County: Conditions and Needs.* Miami: October 1972.

Metropolitan Dade County Planning Department. *Metropolitan Development Policies,* Part 1 of the *Comprehensive Development Master Plan.* Miami: 1974.

Metropolitan Dade County Planning Department. *Environmental Protection.* Part 2 of the *Comprehensive Development Master Plan.* Miami: 1974.

Metropolitan Dade County Planning Department. *Metropolitan Development.* Part 3 of the *Comprehensive Development Master Plan,* Miami: 1974.

Metropolitan Dade County County Planning Department and Metropolitan Dade County Ports and Recreation Department. *Open Space and Recreation.* Proposed Master Plan for Dade County, Florida. Miami: 1969.

Metropolitan Dade County Planning Department, Research Division, "The Retirement World of Miami (Dade County)." Miami, October 1973.

Park, Robert E.; Burgess, Ernest W. and McKenzie, Roderick D., eds. *The City.* Chicago: The University of Chicago Press, 1925.

Pollack, Kent. "Plight of the Older American: Losing Battles on Many Fronts." *The Miami Herald*, April 30, 1974, pp. 1D and 3D.

Rose, Harold M. *The Black Ghetto: A Spatial Behavioral Perspective.* New York: McGraw Hill, 1971.

Salter, Paul S., and Mings, Robert C. "The Projected Impact of Cuban Settlement on Voting Patterns in Metropolitan Miami" *The Professional Geographer* 24, 2 (May 1972).

Sofen, Edward. *The Miami Metropolitan Experiment.* 2nd ed. Garden City, N.Y.: Doubleday Anchor, 1966.

About the Authors

David B. Longbrake received his B.A. from Carroll College, his M.A. from the University of Chicago, and his Ph.D. from the University of Iowa. Dr. Longbrake is presently an Assistant Professor teaching courses in urban geography and urban and regional planning at the University of Miami. He has also held positions in urban and regional planning and has served in various capacities as a planning consultant including Vice-President of Sorensen and Associates.

Woodrow W. Nichols, Jr. is Assoicate Professor and Chairman of Geography at North Carolina Central University. He received his B.A. degree from North Carolina Central University, M.A. degree from Michigan State University, and the Ph.D. degree from the University of California at Los Angeles. He has held teaching posts at Livingstone College, Johnson C. Smith University, California State University at Los Angeles, and the University of Miami. Professor Nichols specializes in urban geography and is a member of the Commission on Geography and Afro-America.